Deciphering Dressage

Deciphering Dressage

KAREN LEIGH DAVIS

Howell Book House
Published by Wiley Publishing, Inc., Hoboken, New Jersey

Photo credits: Page 6 courtesy of Alice Alley. Page 75 courtesy of Marilou Black. Pages 130, 192, 221, and 224 courtesy of Michael and Marie Klimchuk. Pages 3, 214, and 217 courtesy of Anne Medina and Holly Veloso. All other photographs are the author's.

For general information on our other products and services or to obtain technical support please contact our Customer Care Department within the U.S. at (800) 762-2974, outside the U.S. at (317) 572-3993 or fax (317) 572-4002.

Wiley also publishes its books in a variety of electronic formats. Some content that appears in print may not be available in electronic books. For more information about Wiley products, please visit our web site at www.wiley.com.

Library of Congress Cataloging-in-Publication Data:

Davis, Karen Leigh, date.
Deciphering dressage / Karen Davis.— 1st ed.
p. cm.
Includes bibliographical references and index.
ISBN-10: 0-7645-7820-0 (cloth)
ISBN-13: 978-0-7645-7820-5 (cloth)
1. Dressage. I. Title.
SF309.5.D36 2005
798.2'3—dc22 2005007308

Printed in the United States of America

10 9 8 7 6 5 4 3 2 1

Book design by Scott Meola, with Melissa Auciello-Brogan and Beth Brooks
Cover design by Wendy Mount
Book production by Wiley Publishing, Inc. Composition Services

Contents

Preface

Classical dressage is widely recognized around the world for turning out the best riders because of its emphasis on correct training. But what is it? While it's been practiced for centuries in European countries, dressage is a relatively new equestrian discipline in the United States, having arrived here only within the last three decades or so. A lot of people have either never heard of it, or they perceive it as fancy tricks taught for exhibition, but with no practical purpose for the ordinary horse and rider.

Once, an acquaintance of mine learned that I had horses and asked whether I rode English or Western. I explained that I was a dressage rider. To my surprise, her eyes flew open wide and she said in a rather awestruck tone, "Oh, you're a *real* rider!"

Her statement made me realize how others perceive dressage, and even how some riders may consider dressage beyond their reach or their financial means. Nothing could be more untrue. Dressage is something that every horse and rider can benefit from. If you pursue it with a committed spirit, the classical principles will, in time, mold you into a *correct* rider who can train his own horse. To train a horse properly, you must first learn to ride correctly.

To that end, I want to clarify that this book is not intended as a riding instruction manual. You will not read about how to execute the half-pass or flying changes here. There are many fine books on the market that thoroughly cover these topics and more, and I've provided a comprehensive list in the back of this book for your reading reference.

I also want to clarify that I am neither an expert rider nor an expert trainer in the field of dressage. Some people think that if you've written a book on a subject, then you must be an expert on something. But I am just an ordinary riding student, perhaps just like you, who has studied dressage for many years, seeking to become the best rider and horseman I can possibly be. If I'm an expert at anything, it's in knowing what the pitfalls are along this journey, because I've encountered them all at one time or another. I would probably be a lot further along in my quest if I had known then, when I started, what I know now.

The knowledge I've gained along the way is what I hope to share with you within these pages, so that your journey may be a little smoother. This book is intended as a student primer of sorts and provides some advice on how to start your journey and tips about what to expect along the way. Whether you've been riding in other equestrian disciplines for awhile, or just getting acquainted with horses, I hope this book will help you decipher your future riding goals and aspirations.

For all those spouses and spectators who accompany their dressage fanatic friends and family members to horse shows, this book is also intended to help you decipher what you're watching at such an event. Although it's easy to appreciate the fluid grace and beauty of the upper-level dressage movements, the more you know about them, the more enjoyable this sport becomes.

Acknowledgments

I would like to thank my riding instructors, Holly Veloso, and her mother, Judy Westenhoefer, for helping me realize many of my dressage goals. I further thank Holly for her willingness to be photographed for this book, demonstrating both correct and incorrect riding positions and movements. Holly appears riding Grande American, affectionately known as Ami, an Intermediate level Hanoverian mare, owned and trained by Judy.

I also thank the following friends and fellow riding students who donated photographs for the book, appeared in photographs, or allowed their horses to be photographed: Marilou Black, Lindsay Black, Michael and Marie Klimchuk, Annette Medina, Karen Russell, and Samantha Veloso. Thanks also to the many friends and associates of the Southwest Virginia Dressage Association for sharing their collective knowledge and camaraderie and for sponsoring educational opportunities that have helped me grow in this sport.

Finally, I am thankful to have had the opportunity to learn on such excellent schoolmasters as Ami and my own mare, Windspiel. After all, horses can be our best teachers, if we would just learn to listen to what they're telling us.

Chapter One

What Is Dressage?

Dressage Defined

When I tell someone, "I'm a dressage rider," most people, having never heard the word *dressage*, have no idea what I'm talking about. The term *classical riding* typically draws the same response. Often, I try to explain it as *precision riding*, but this definition falls short, too, because dressage is so much more than just a riding discipline. Dressage is really a humane and wholesome philosophy of horsemanship that honors and encompasses every aspect of the horse-human relationship.

Many people think dressage is trick riding because of the fancy, dance-like maneuvers that trained dressage horses can perform. But dressage maneuvers are not tricks. They are polished enhancements of natural movements that all horses can execute when romping with their pasture mates. Watch a herd of horses prancing about at play and you'll likely see a series of flying changes, pirouettes, maybe even a little passage or extended trot, and sometimes the spectacular leaps referred to as airs above the ground. Later in the book, I'll explain what these terms mean, but first, let's talk about what dressage is.

A Training Method

Viewed as the ultimate approach to achieving harmony between horse and rider, the art of classical riding, called dressage, is centuries old, with roots traced as far back as the fourth century BC. The term *dressage*, pronounced with emphasis on the second syllable (dres-SASSH), stems from the French word for *training.* By definition, it is a systematic approach to training and athletically conditioning the horse by gradually schooling the animal through a series of gymnastic-like movements at progressive levels. Each level builds on the previous one, conditioning and preparing the horse physically and mentally for the more difficult and challenging maneuvers ahead.

Dressage fosters harmony and communication between horse and rider because results are achieved through careful insight and cooperation rather than coercion or force. Through dressage training, nearly every horse can be improved and molded into a happier, safer, more reliable, and ultimately more marketable mount.

During a dressage test or exhibition (see the figure on the next page), horse and rider execute intricate patterns and transitions from one gait to another that flow like a dance. Sometimes this dance is set to music, which is why people often describe dressage as a beautiful ballet on horseback.

Training begins at the Introductory Level and progresses through to the Olympic ideal, the Grand Prix, the highest level of dressage competition. Of course, not all horses (or riders) are capable of reaching the higher levels of dressage, but any horse can be improved by applying the basic principles to its schooling routine. Likewise, riders who pursue the study of dressage become better riders and trainers because they gain an understanding of the physics and mechanics of riding. Ultimately, dressage aims to make the horse more freely forward moving, straight, supple, balanced, collected, relaxed, and obedient, and the rider more attuned to his mount.

A Riding Foundation

The foundation of all riding on the flat, dressage principles can apply to and enhance work in any equestrian discipline or breed, including jumping, western and gaited horses. The exercises and patterns help improve the horse's overall balance and athleticism, enabling him to perform better in his current field. Horses that

A dressage test begins with a salute to the judge.

have had some dressage training also become more responsive to their riders' aids, making them more pleasurable to ride.

Dressage also trains the rider to sit the horse correctly, using light, effective, balanced, and nonabusive aids or signals that cue the horse to execute a specific gait or movement. When performed at its best, dressage looks effortless and unconstrained to observers as the horse moves fluidly through his paces in response to barely perceptible signals from his rider. So subtle are the aids that the rider appears to sit motionless in the saddle, as if willing the horse to do all the work. Such effective communication without force and tension should be what every rider strives for, regardless of the chosen sport or discipline.

Without question, dressage is the most difficult and demanding of all the equestrian disciplines, yet any rider can participate on any horse or pony, purebred or not, and benefit from work at the lower levels. Even mules can participate at certain shows.

Dressage appeals to many riders who appreciate a challenge but do not relish the risky, daredevil nature of jumping or eventing. It also appeals more to people who start riding as adults because they can pursue it at their own pace and, health permitting, continue enjoying riding well into their later years. You do not necessarily have to be young, slim, trim, and athletically inclined to participate in the sport, although it helps! The longer and more frequently you ride, the more physically fit you will become over time, because riding is strenuous aerobic exercise, despite the misconceptions of many unfamiliar with it.

Dressage is also for people who like learning for the sake of learning, because it truly is an in-depth study of the physics and philosophy of riding, encompassing both the art and science of horsemanship. Whether pursued to the higher levels for its own sake or as basic training in preparation for other equestrian activities, dressage offers the best education a horse and rider can receive.

A Competitive Sport

In dressage competition, the ongoing education of horse and rider is tested at each level of development. This is why a dressage show is unlike any other horse show. At most horse shows, multiple riders enter the show ring at one time and compete at various paces before the judge. At a dressage show, a single horse-and-rider team enters the arena to perform a given test, depending on their current level of training. A test consists of patterns and transitions performed in a certain order within a rectangular arena marked with letters. The letters assist the rider in knowing when and where to execute a particular movement. Each movement receives a score from 1 to 10. The better the performance, the more points are tallied.

To someone who does not ride, a dressage test can be difficult to understand or evaluate. People who ride understand the complexity of the cues used to tell the horse what to do, but nonriders lack this appreciation. This is why dressage is not a great spectator sport, particularly at the lower levels. Typically, it takes a well-trained eye to distinguish the nuances that separate a so-so ride from a terrific one. Dressage at the higher levels is easier for the layperson to appreciate because the degree of difficulty in upper-level movements, such as the passage and piaffe, is more evident. Also, by this time in his training the horse has achieved greater collection, grace, and beauty in his paces and is a pleasure to watch. The most brilliant horse-and-rider teams surpass sport and approach the realm of art, which can be enjoyed by all.

An Equestrian Art

The study of dressage does not require you to compete at horse shows. In the history of the world's greatest dressage masters, some never competed, but preferred instead to pursue it as an art form. Competition does, however, enable the rider to measure her progress and ability against other riders at the same level.

The harmony of unspoken language between horse and rider and the pursuit of perfection and unity truly elevates dressage from mere sport to equestrian art form. Dressage as an art is preserved in its purest form and performed in its finest tradition by the famous Lipizzaners of the Spanish Riding School in Vienna, Austria. Besides standard dressage movements and quadrilles, the Lipizzaner stallions perform stunning leaps, called airs above the ground, which are a part of classical equestrian art. The airs, however, are not featured in today's dressage competitions, as few horses are capable of performing them.

A Personal Journey

For the rider who pursues classical riding as an art, rather than as a mere sport or recreation, dressage becomes a passion, a lifestyle, and often a journey of self-discovery. Success in dressage demands true self-discipline, attention to details, and a sound work ethic. It involves developing a profound awareness of your own body in relation to each move the horse makes. It involves learning how to care for and communicate with another species. It involves analyzing training obstacles, finding creative solutions, and sometimes facing your own fears and limitations. It involves studying and accumulating an array of knowledge in topics such as horse care and nutrition, veterinary medicine, hoof care, equine behavior, pasture maintenance, tack selection, sports psychology, and much more.

Holly Veloso rides a test on Grande American, owned and trained by Judy Westenhoefer.

Most of all, dressage demands patience and perseverance. Any ideal of perfection takes years of training to achieve, and there are no shortcuts, even though some have been tried with less-than-perfect results. Moving through each level is a painstaking progression for both horse and rider, often riddled with setbacks and frustration. Classical principles have been time tested by riding masters throughout the centuries. Their enduring wisdom dictates that the horse cannot be rushed or forced into attempting any movement that he is not ready to do. To do so only creates tension in the animal and ultimately inhibits the grace and beauty of the movement.

For the rider who perseveres, the payoff is well worth the effort. The privilege and experience of riding an upper-level, classically trained horse elicits a natural high like no other. The horse in motion feels like it is floating forward effortlessly, each hoof barely striking the ground. The rider feels a sensation of great ease and confidence in the saddle, as if all she need do is think the movement and the horse responds accordingly, as shown in the figure on the previous page. The intimate communication and horse-human bond necessary to execute the movements is extraordinarily fulfilling. This is true partnership achieved.

For all of these reasons, dressage is truly challenging to pursue, but just as intensely satisfying and rewarding. In learning to ride well in this sport, we must learn self-discipline and confront our own riding fears and limitations. By learning to train our horses as we ride, we discover the boundaries of our personal patience, our emotional liabilities, and most of all a deep sense of awe at our acquired ability to communicate in an unspoken language with another species.

A Common-Sense Science

Dressage can mean many things to many people: a training method, a riding discipline, a foundation for other riding activities, a competitive sport, or an equestrian art. The term *classical riding* conjures up images of pomp and pageantry, probably because traditional dressage exhibitions sometimes involve a great deal of ostentation as horse and rider take to their dance floor, the dressage arena, and strut their steps. For some people, this image makes dressage seem unattainable. But the truth is, dressage is simply common-sense riding, as Sylvia

Loch so eloquently states it in her book, *The Classical Rider: Being at One with Your Horse.*

Once you begin seriously studying dressage principles, it becomes evident how common sense has fashioned the classical techniques. They are solidly founded on the physics and mechanics of the horse's gaits and movements. There is sound reason for why the riding aids are applied a certain way for each movement. When used correctly, they are both effective and humane. This makes dressage as much a science as an art. The rider who fully grasps the concepts and understands not only how but, more important, why the aids are applied a certain way truly becomes a thinking rider who can effectively troubleshoot training obstacles and behavior problems.

This acquired knowledge and discipline is important, because each time you ride a horse, you essentially are training it. Depending on your own riding skills, you may teach your horse either good or bad habits. For example, if you allow the horse to move off on its own while you are mounting, you teach the horse that this is okay. For safety's sake, however, you must not allow the horse to anticipate your next move and act on its own. You must always insist that the horse stand still until you are securely seated in the saddle, and then move off only on your command. This seems like common sense, but it is surprising how many sloppy riders overlook simple issues like this every time they ride. Then they wonder why their horses develop such naughty habits.

A thinking rider is always in control, aware of the slightest deviation from the desired direction of movement, and ready to make small corrections as needed without force. A knowledgeable rider also understands and respects the horse's current conditioning and abilities and does not ask him to do more than he is capable of doing. Such careful and thoughtful handling teaches the horse to trust and rely on his rider. When faced with a frightening situation, a horse handled this way is more likely to look to his rider for safety and obey the commands he is given. This is what good common-sense training is all about: creating an equine companion that is safe and pleasurable to ride.

A Brief History of Dressage

Dressage has existed as a system of training in other parts of the world for centuries, but didn't land on American soil until about thirty years ago. In some European countries, top-level dressage horses are revered as national treasures, and Olympic-class dressage riders are as celebrated as popular football and basketball players are in the United States.

Ancient Origins

Historians generally credit a Greek military man named Xenophon, who lived in the fourth century BC, as the founder of classical equitation. He wrote the oldest known surviving horsemanship manual, outlining humane training principles, of which many remain valid today. In his treatise, Xenophon describes how a deep, balanced seat and slight shifts in the rider's weight can be used to signal and collect the horse for precision movements. Precision riding was a necessary skill in Xenophon's time, as war horses trained for battle needed to be easily maneuverable and ultraresponsive to their rider's commands. They had to be able to turn or wheel about swiftly while maintaining balance. Often, the rider's hands were occupied with sword and shield, therefore, the legs, seat, and weight were the primary tools of influence, and well-trained horses were fine-tuned to these aids.

Xenophon's style of sitting a horse, as if standing with legs apart, rather than sitting as if in a chair, would later be refined and become known as the classical seat. If you observe today's top dressage riders, you will note that they ride with a long, nearly straight leg, knee slightly bent, and with a vertical, upright position, as if almost standing in the stirrups.

What's interesting, however, is that in Xenophon's time the stirrup had not been invented. Riders in those days obviously possessed extraordinary balance. Following the lessons of history, today's riders realize the value in riding without stirrups and routinely drop their irons during practice to help develop better balance and body position.

Combined Training

The classical seat differs from the more familiar forward seat or hunt seat position used for jumping (see the following figure). The English jumping saddle is designed with the flaps extending forward to help support the rider's more forward-leaning position. Dressage saddle (shown on the next page) flaps drop straight down to accommodate the rider's straighter leg and a more centered position.

Each style of riding has its place and purpose, yet even the best hunt seat riders employ the virtues of the classical seat during flatwork exercises to collect and supple their horses. Such cross-training benefits both horse and rider and is the basis for eventing, which combines the disciplines of dressage, cross-country, and stadium jumping. Riders who participate in all three sports practice what is commonly referred to as combined training.

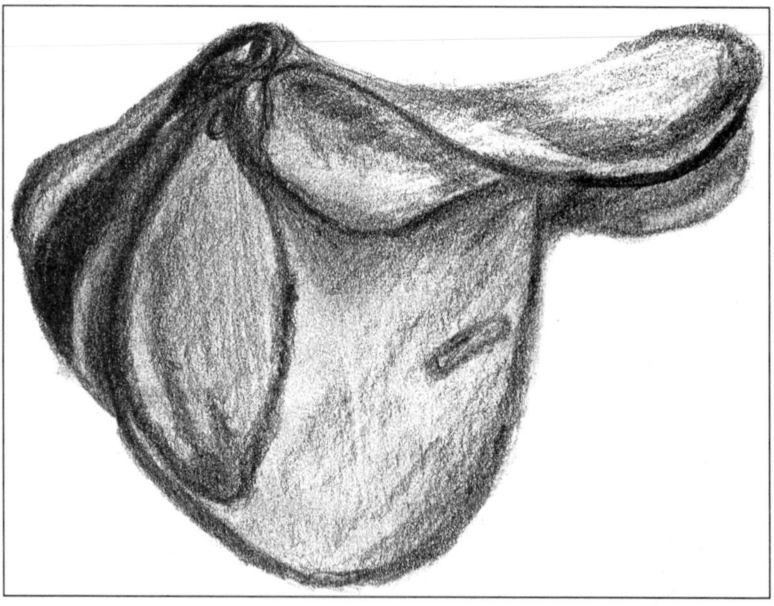

The forward seat saddle used for jumping has flaps extending forward to support the rider's more forward-leaning position.

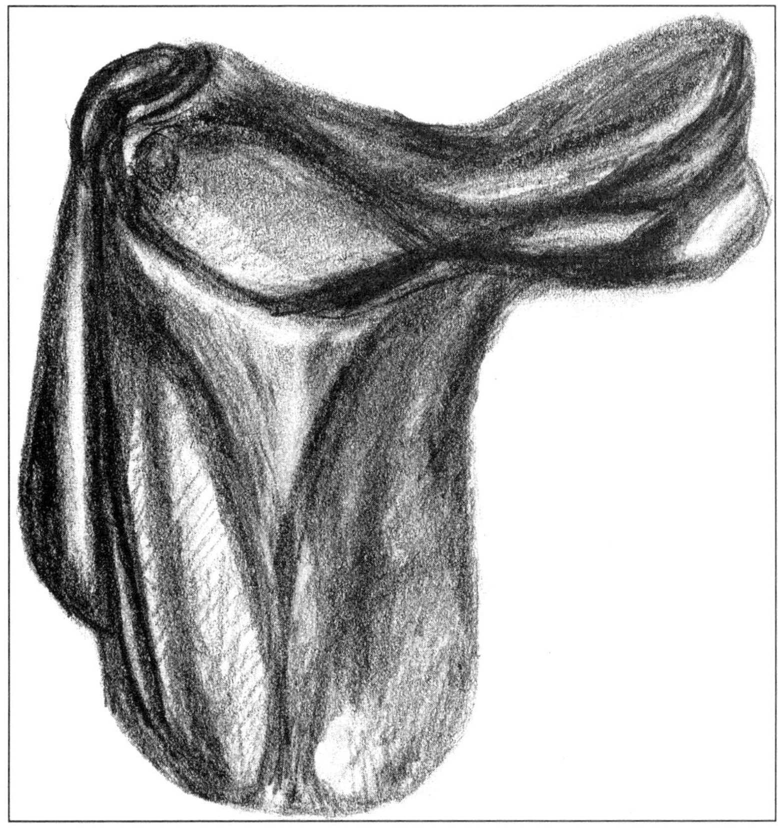

The dressage saddle has longer flaps that drop straight down to accommodate the dressage rider's straighter leg and upright position.

Cavalry Competition

For centuries, classical equitation remained the domain of the European aristocracy and the cavalry. It is, perhaps, a sad commentary on humanity that such a beautiful art form arose from the need for responsive war horses. Competitive dressage was even introduced as a military competition in the 1912 Olympics in Stockholm, Sweden. At that time, the tests for cavalry officers and their horses included jumping and barely resembled the tests we know today in Grand Prix dressage. Civilians were not allowed to participate until the 1950s.

American Dressage

In the United States, where western, gaited, and jumping horses have predominated, dressage was practically unheard of until the early 1970s. Before that decade, the average American's exposure to anything even remotely resembling dressage was at the circus. There were, however, a few riders and trainers trying to stir interest in the sport. Most had European connections.

One of the primary movers and shakers was the former Olympian Colonel Bengt Ljungquist, who came from Sweden to settle and teach in Maryland. Ljungquist coached several riders who later became international competitors. In 1974, he became the dressage coach for the U.S. Equestrian Team. After his leadership landed a bronze medal for the U.S. team at the 1976 Olympics in Montreal, Canada, American interest in dressage began to escalate. Women riders especially took note because the winning U.S. team was composed of three women: Hilda Gurney aboard Keen, Dorothy Morkis on Monaco, and Edith Master riding Dahlwitz. Today, American membership in the sport remains overwhelmingly dominated by female participants.

Meanwhile, the U.S. Dressage Federation (USDF) was founded in 1973 to foster dressage growth in this country. Its efforts proved successful, as dressage soon became the fastest growing equestrian sport in the nation. After its 1973 founding, the USDF signed up about 2,800 individual members and 25 dressage clubs, called group-member organizations (GMOs). By 2005, there were about 33,000 individual members and 130 GMOs. Within this thirty-year span, the number of recognized competitions jumped from just 34 to 787.

How Dressage Competitions Are Governed

If dressage competition interests you, you need to know how shows are organized and governed. Your best source of information is the *Rule Book*, which is published annually by the U.S. Equestrian Federation (USEF), the national governing body of equestrian competition, formerly known as the American Horse Shows Association. The *Rule Book*'s dressage section provides detailed information on the following:

- The governing rules and regulations
- General principles of dressage
- Descriptions and requirements of the gaits and movements
- Descriptions and requirements of the dressage levels
- Requirements of the dressage tests
- The figures and exercises
- Dress and saddlery requirements
- Drawings of bits permitted in competition
- Prize and awards information
- Who the show officials are
- Information about qualifying and championship classes

Contact information for the USEF and related organizations is provided in the back of this book.

The U.S. Dressage Federation

The USDF promotes dressage interest and education in this country. The USDF works closely with local, regional, and national organizations to accomplish this goal. It is comprised of individual participating members as well as members affiliated through their GMOs (such as dressage clubs) and intercollegiate/interscholastic member organizations.

The USDF also administers a national year-end awards program for every level of competition, based on test scores earned throughout the year. Special categories exist for different breeds, junior/young riders, adult amateur riders, and riders aged 50 and older.

The USDF lists ten regions on its Web site at www.usdf.org. Each region has a GMO List, where you can click to obtain a list of the group member organizations nearest you and their contact information.

Region 1: Delaware, Maryland, New Jersey, North Carolina, Pennsylvania, Virginia, eastern West Virginia, and Washington, D.C.

Region 2: Illinois, Indiana, Kentucky, Michigan, Ohio, West Virginia, and Wisconsin

Region 3: Alabama, Florida, Georgia, South Carolina, and Tennessee

Region 4: Iowa, Kansas, Minnesota, Missouri, Nebraska, North Dakota, and South Dakota

Region 5: Arizona, Colorado, eastern Montana, New Mexico, Utah, western Texas, and Wyoming

Region 6: Alaska, Idaho, western Montana, Oregon, and Washington

Region 7: California, Hawaii, and Nevada

Region 8: Connecticut, Maine, Massachusetts, New Hampshire, New York, Rhode Island, and Vermont

Region 9: Arkansas, Louisiana, Mississippi, Oklahoma, and Texas

Region 10: International

Types of Dressage Shows

While large all-breed horse shows may sometimes offer dressage divisions, most dressage shows are limited exclusively to dressage classes. These are further divided into recognized or schooling shows. Both types of shows are typically organized by a USDF-affiliated dressage club chapter or GMO and afford ample opportunities for volunteers to help out and learn every aspect of how a horse show is managed.

Recognized Shows

A *recognized show* simply means that the show organizers and exhibitors have paid the required fees to the national governing body, the USEF, and agree to abide by all USEF rules and regulations. Riders of all levels from various areas may compete in recognized, or rated, shows to accumulate awards and points toward state or regional qualifications. Once a horse has earned the required qualifying scores, it is eligible to compete in regional championships. The USDF also awards gold, silver, and bronze medals to those who achieve the required scores.

Schooling Shows

Schooling shows, or nonrated shows, are where most people start competing at the lower levels to gain experience and learn show protocol. These shows are more casual and loosely organized and are usually less stringent about rule enforcement than recognized shows. In addition, the entry fees are typically lower because schooling shows are not required to hire licensed judges.

As the name implies, schooling shows give novice or beginning dressage riders a chance to learn, experiment, and practice their tests and experience a competitive atmosphere without the pressures of a recognized show. Schooling shows are also ideal venues for introducing a young, green horse to the sights and sounds of the show arena. Often, horse and rider may perform well at home but fall apart under pressure at shows. It is common for horses, especially young, inexperienced ones, to become easily distracted or nervous in unfamiliar territory. Schooling shows provide an opportunity to discover and deal with these situations before moving on to the more competitive atmosphere of recognized shows.

Ride-a-Tests

Ride-a-tests are even more informal than schooling shows and provide an additional opportunity for horse and rider to practice a test and get a taste of what a real show is like, before actually entering one. Because ride-a-tests are pretend shows—that is, loosely organized local events that are not subject to the usual rules and regulations—organizers generally attempt to adhere to them for the sake of practice. Ride-a-tests typically are organized independently by a riding club or facility for its members and judged by a local trainer or instructor.

Eventing or Combined Training Competitions

Eventing, or combined training competitions, are sanctioned by both the USEF and the U.S. Eventing Association and governed accordingly. These competitions include tests in dressage, jumping, and cross-country and often take place over several days (see "Combined Training" section earlier in this chapter). Dressage at an eventing competition is judged in basically the same manner as regular dressage shows, although there are some variations in the rules, attire, tack, and protocol. Many eventing judges are also licensed as dressage judges.

The National Governing Body

The USDF works closely with the equestrian national governing body (NGB) to help develop the dressage tests used in competitions. The tests are revised every four years to accommodate changes and the natural evolution that occurs in competitive sports.

For years, the American Horse Shows Association, which later was renamed USA Equestrian, set the rules and regulations governing recognized shows in the United States. In 2003, however, a new equestrian NGB officially began operations. The new NGB, formally called the U.S. Equestrian Federation, was created by merging USA Equestrian with the U.S. Equestrian Team. Headquartered in Lexington, Kentucky, at the prestigious Kentucky Horse Park, the new NGB sets rules and standards, writes national tests, and governs the conduct of horse shows nationwide.

The Federation Equestre Internationale

The Federation Equestre Internationale (FEI) is the international governing body for all Olympic equestrian games worldwide and international-caliber dressage events. The *FEI levels* refer to the Prix St. Georges, Intermediate I, Intermediate II, and Grand Prix international levels of competition.

Here's what the FEI levels mean:

- Prix St. Georges follows Fourth Level and represents the medium stage of training.
- Intermediate I represents a more advanced stage of training than Prix St. Georges.
- Intermediate II, also an advanced stage of training, exists primarily to prepare the horse for the Grand Prix level.
- Grand Prix is the highest level of competition.

While the FEI regulates dressage competition worldwide, each country has its own national governing body—the aforementioned USEF being the NGB for the United States. The FEI designs the tests and sets standards for the higher levels of competition, while the USEF and USDF work together in this country to develop tests for the lower levels, closely following FEI directives and recommendations.

Chapter Two

The Discipline of Dressage

An Overview of the Rider's Aids

As a riding discipline, dressage is all about communication between horse and rider. The cues, commands, or body signals that humans have devised to help the horse understand what we want are called the aids. The natural aids the rider uses to converse with his horse are the hands, legs, seat, and voice. The artificial aids, which help reinforce the natural aids, are the whip and spur. When used to make the horse go forward, the commands are called the driving aids. The aids are basically the same in all equestrian disciplines, with slight variations, whether you're riding English or Western, jumping horses or reining horses.

Despite the reality that you can use almost any set of cues to teach a horse something, the aids are remarkably uniform among horsemen worldwide, although each rider tends to adapt them to his own way of communicating with his horse. This is because the aids are basically applied physical science. Centuries ago, discerning trainers figured out that horses respond to pressure in predictable ways and used that knowledge to their advantage. For example, if you stand beside a horse and gently poke your finger into his side at about the same place where the rider's leg hangs, he will step sideways, away from the pressure of your touch. Through trial and error, horsemen of long ago discovered the right *buttons* that make the horse stop and go or execute lateral movements. Fortunately, they handed down their collective knowledge in the body of classical riding literature that we have today.

Simply speaking, applying the aids is a matter of pushing the right buttons to elicit the desired response. In dressage, the rider learns to apply and coordinate the aids with a high degree of precision and sensitivity, making the aids seem nearly invisible to onlookers. Although truly working hard in the saddle, the best dressage riders make the sport look effortless, as if the horse is doing all the work, and the rider is astride merely to enjoy the ride.

This quiet, balanced coordination of the aids is a skill that takes good coaching and countless hours in the saddle to perfect. Although the aids may be simple in principle, their correct application is an intricate interplay of precise timing and body control. Before the rider can influence the horse well with the aids, he must first learn to sit still in the saddle, without bouncing or letting his arms and legs flap loosely about. If you observe the best dressage riders, they appear to sit motionless on the horse. In reality, the entire body moves fluidly in concert with the horse's rhythm, so that the motion of both beings blends into one. To ride this way requires the rider to achieve a state of attentive relaxation from head to toe, while maintaining precise control over how his body parts and weight distribution influence the horse. Horse and rider practice and train for years to achieve this harmonious oneness and communication that makes their brief performance in the dressage arena appear effortless, fluid, and beautiful. While good riders may make it look easy, dressage is widely considered the most difficult of all the riding disciplines.

Your Hands

Of the natural aids, the hands are probably less important than the seat and legs in dressage (see the figures on pages 20 and 21), yet they can be the most abusive when used thoughtlessly. Novice riders tend to hang onto the reins for balance until they learn how to sit the horse properly and develop a secure seat. For riders who fail to receive good instruction, balancing off the hands can become a bad and dangerous habit that's hard to break. The rider who persistently balances off the reins, which is uncomfortable to the horse's mouth, often unwittingly creates behavioral problems in his mount, which wants only to escape his rider's abusive hands by any means possible.

Correct hands: The reins run between the last two fingers, the wrists face each other, the thumbs rest on top of the reins, and the fingers curl lightly around them with a firm grip.

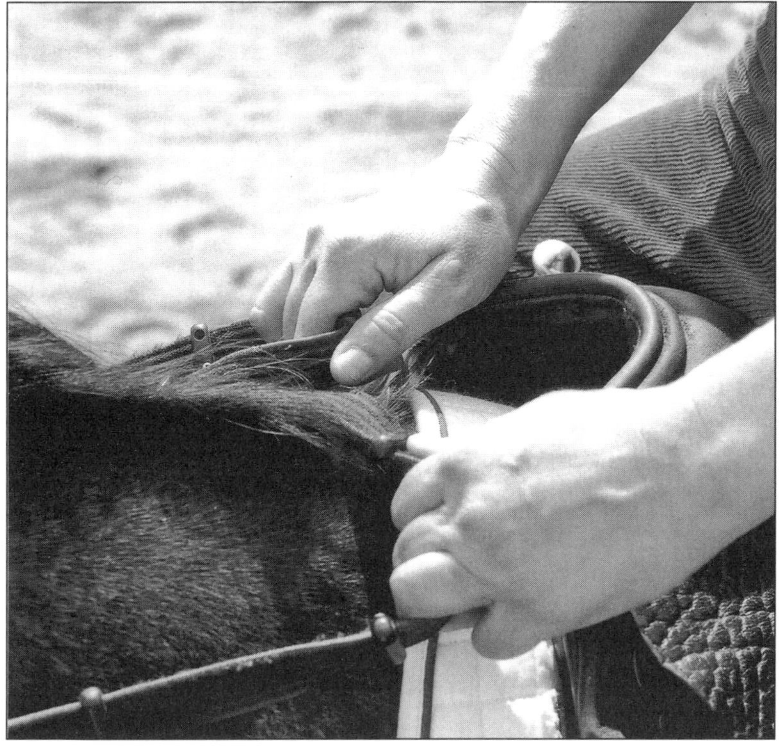

Incorrect hands: Flat hands, where the wrists turn downward, are ineffective and a common fault.

Contact

Dressage teaches the rider to take a soft, elastic contact on the reins. Contact is the connection between the horse's mouth and the rider's hands. The rider bends his elbows and holds his hands such that a straight line of communication travels from the bit in the horse's mouth to the rider's hands. The reins are neither slack nor excessively taut. The rider's fingers close firmly around the reins, wrists and palms face each other about a handcuff length apart, and thumbs rest on top.

The rider squeezes or releases the fingers to varying degrees to regulate the contact and to talk to the horse. A slight turn of the wrist can signal a change in direction. Sensitive riders keep up a running conversation with their horses in this way, gently working and massaging the reins while going through their paces. The amount of aid needed varies for every rider, every horse, and every movement, and it takes lots of practice to develop good hands, to know when the contact feels right, and to be able to make adjustments without yanking the horse's mouth.

Some people hear the phrases *soft contact* and *lightness in the bridle* and mistake them to mean a loose rein, but this is not the case at all. By necessity, the rider's hold on the reins may need to be firm, but the contact is said to be soft when the rider's hands are communicating in an effective, sensitive, and nonabusive manner with the horse's mouth.

Lightness has nothing to do with rein tension. It is a component of the horse's self-carriage, achieved when the horse is engaged, collected, and moving forward into the bridle by pushing off from his hindquarters. When a horse moves in this manner, he carries more of his weight on the back end, rather than on the forehand, and consequently feels light in the bridle to his rider.

The opposite is a horse that carries more of his weight on the forehand, a condition referred to as heavy on the forehand or falling on the forehand. When riding a horse that moves in this manner, the rider experiences the heavy, unpleasant sensation of trying to hold the horse's front end up by the reins. Proper dressage training and riding can help correct this fault, although some horses' conformation, or body build, predisposes them to the tendency to move off the forehand.

Control

Most people think the hands and reins are the steering wheel and the brakes. We've all seen those old Westerns where the cowboy gallops his horse into town, hauls back hard on the reins as the horse flings his head high in the air, and skids to a stop with hindquarters strung out well behind. This may make a dramatic entrance, but the guy would flunk a dressage test before he even had a chance to salute.

Simply pulling back on the reins to halt is crude and incorrect, and usually causes the horse to throw up his head in discomfort and come off contact. Aside from making the horse unhappy, this is neither a safe nor an effective way to ride. Coming off contact equals a loss of control for the rider, because that straight line of communication from the horse's mouth to the rider's hands is broken. A horse that's off the bit can more easily misbehave or bolt, and given the opportunity, why wouldn't he, when his rider has caused him such discomfort?

The reins do not act alone as steering wheel and brakes. Used in conjunction with the other natural driving aids, the legs and seat, the reins guide the horse and hold him in a frame. The rider uses his whole body—hand, legs, seat, and weight—to influence the horse's movement. For example, to slow or stop the horse correctly, the rider applies the following sequence of aids almost simultaneously:

1. He sits back more deeply and heavily in the saddle.
2. He drives the horse forward into the bit from the legs and seat, pushing slightly more from the inside leg into a firm and steady outside rein.
3. He momentarily stops moving his body with the horse's motion.
4. He closes his fingers more firmly on the reins and resists further forward motion with his hands, holding rather than pulling back.
5. He releases the holding pressure when the horse stops.

As this carefully choreographed sequence of aids clearly demonstrates, proper riding technique requires more skill and finesse than just kicking the horse to go and hauling back on the reins to stop. While it's true that anyone can get on and force the horse to go and stop in this crude and cruel fashion, it takes a carefully trained rider to do it correctly, without creating resentment, resistance, and discomfort in the horse. To progress up the levels in dressage and achieve that ballet-like lightness so sought after in the sport, riders must learn to use their aids in concert—their whole body in perfect control, not just the hands.

The Rein Effects

The reins can be used in several ways to influence the horse's direction and positioning, but it takes a lot of practice for a rider to master and apply the nuances of the different effects with great precision.

The Opening or Leading Rein

Generally, the rider holds the reins close to or touching the horse's neck. To use an opening rein, the rider shifts one hand slightly away from the neck without pulling back on it. This has the effect of leading the horse's nose toward the direction the rider wants him to take.

The Neck Rein

Neck reining is usually associated with western horses, but all well-trained dressage horses will neck rein, too. For example, when the rider places the right rein against the base of the horse's neck, the horse's natural tendency is to step to the left, away from that slight rein pressure.

The Reins of Opposition

When the rider uses the reins of opposition, he indirectly influences movement of the hindquarters by placing the reins in such a way as to oppose movement of the shoulders, so that the horse has no choice but to step with his hindquarters in the desired direction. The effect is different depending on whether the rider holds the rein straight (direct rein of opposition), or lays it against the horse's neck in front of the withers or behind the withers for a neck-reining effect.

The Leg Aids

Think of the leg aids as the accelerator, one of the driving aids. They initiate forward movement. The legs also help bend the horse in turns and on circles, for example. Hanging quietly at the horse's side, the leg can also provide support and prevent the hindquarters from swinging out to the side.

The rider's legs should wrap around the horse's barrel like a wet dish rag, but not flopping. The toes should be pointed forward, not angled out to the side, which is a common fault. The lower legs (from the knees down) stay in close contact with the saddle, but do not grip constantly, as some insecure riders develop a bad habit of doing. The thighs hang open and relaxed from the hips, resting with contact against the saddle but not gripping or pinching. The rider must learn to work the lower legs independently of the upper legs to apply the aids, but he cannot do so effectively if he hangs on at the calf, knee, or thigh with a viselike death grip.

Depending on the desired result, the leg aids may be applied at points on the girth or behind the girth with varying pressure and intensity. The horse's natural response is to step away from the pressure. Therefore, if the rider presses his right leg against the horse's right side, the horse will step to the left, and vice versa. The rider may apply one leg or the other in this way to ask the horse to step sideways, for example.

When the rider presses both legs evenly against the horse's sides, the horse moves away from the pressure by stepping forward between the legs. The harder you squeeze, the faster the horse goes. The faster the horse goes, the more tightly most beginning riders instinctively grip with the legs, which serves only to urge the horse on more. In such a situation, an uneducated rider often blames his horse for being disobedient by speeding up, when it is really the rider's lack of skill and failure to use well-balanced aids to regulate the pace and maintain control.

When applying the driving aids, good dressage instructors teach you from the outset to ride your horse from back to front into contact. That is, apply the leg and seat aids first to engage the hindquarters, then use the hands to steer the forehand and regulate the pace. Basically, the hands control the front end, while the legs keep the rear in gear, in acceleration mode. Think of the horse as being two halves: the front end and the back end.

The rider's job is to keep both ends connected and working together. Simply speaking, this is accomplished by driving the hind end toward the front end. Imagine the horse's hind end as his engine. His forward thrust and power comes from the hind legs pushing off, and the front end then directs and carries that momentum onward.

When the push comes from the hindquarters, the front end moves forward more freely and lightly and is easier to steer. This is because the horse must shift his weight back toward his hind end in order to push off effectively from behind. If you ride from front to back, that is, merely steering with the hands without engaging the hindquarters to do the pushing, you allow the front end to drag the back end along. This creates a dragging feel and look to the movement, and the horse is said to be moving on the forehand.

The Seat

More than just your butt in the saddle, the seat is the way the rider sits centered on the horse and uses his vertical position and the weight of his body, as well as his lower back, abdominal muscles, and pelvic bones, to influence his mount's movement. See the figure on the next page. A good seat also gives the rider security. It is the most important aid used in dressage, and for many riders, the hardest to master.

The Classical Seat

The different equitation disciplines employ variations of the seat, depending on what the horse is asked to do. For example, riders of jumping horses use the forward seat or hunt seat, in which the rider leans slightly forward to free the horse's back for jumping. Dressage or classical riding employs the *classical seat*, in which the rider sits straight and upright, perpendicular to the ground, and with shoulders squared back. The legs drop down long and naturally under the body, as if the rider were standing upright, rather than sitting in a chair, except that the knees are slightly bent.

The classical seat is a deep, central seat that is safer because it gives the rider greater balance and control. And because the

Even at rest, this rider is sitting straight and upright, with shoulders squared back, elbows at her side, and leg well back under her.

classical seat helps the rider stay balanced with the horse's movements, it promotes self-carriage in the horse, so that he is freer to perform the more difficult maneuvers required in dressage. The seat aids and their subtle application becomes increasingly important as the horse's training progresses.

Three Points of the Seat

In the classical seat, the rider sits with three points of the pelvic floor touching the saddle. The three points, the left and right seat bones and the crotch or the pubic arch, form a triangle, which is the rider's base of support. To sit flat on this triangle base, the rider must relax and open his thighs from the hip joints as much as possible. The rider's spine retains its natural curve in the lower back. The hips swing with the horse's movements, sparing the rider's spine from excessive jarring while allowing his back muscles to work. Too much tension in the hips, rigidity in the lower back, or clenching with the thighs inhibits good movement and at the faster gaits causes the rider to bounce in the saddle, which is uncomfortable to both horse and rider.

Developing an Independent Seat

It can take some time for the rider to develop a stable seat and learn to feel equal weight on both seat bones. Lessons on the lunge line, without reins and stirrups, are one of the most effective tools for teaching the rider how to maintain his balance on a moving horse and develop an "independent" seat that is not reliant on the hands or legs for stability. Regardless of what style of riding you decide to undertake, you must develop an independent seat to ride well.

After the rider gains stability in the saddle, he can effectively shift his weight more to one seat bone or the other to influence the horse. The rider does not lean his upper body or shift his buttocks sideways to accomplish this, but instead presses down through his leg and heel on the required side, which weights the pelvic seat bone slightly more on that side. This subtle aid causes the horse to step in the direction of the weightier side and is applied in conjunction with other aids when executing turns and lateral movements, such as the half-pass, shoulder-in, travers, and renvers.

Sounds simple, but developing an effective classical seat is one of the most difficult aspects of dressage. The subtlety of the aids demands a great deal of body awareness and control. To communicate effectively through the seat, the rider must become one unit with the horse in a soft, flexible way.

The Forward Seat

As mentioned, the classical seat differs from the forward seat, seen more often with English-style riding and used for jumping or fox hunting. When a rider transfers to dressage from another equestrian discipline, such as hunt seat, learning to sit properly in the classical seat and discerning its nuances and advantages can require considerable practice and additional instruction.

Before I found a dressage instructor in my region and began studying classical riding, I took lessons in saddleseat, a style of equitation used for riding gaited horses, such as American Saddlebreds. Although there are many excellent and effective saddleseat riders, some riders in this discipline incorrectly tend to adopt a chair seat, sitting too far back in the saddle with legs well forward, as if seated on a chair. The saddleseat style also requires riders to ride with their lower leg away from the horse, instead of in close contact with the horse's sides, as you would ride in the classical seat. These are examples of habits that have to be unlearned when switching to dressage and the classical seat.

Later, I experimented with the forward seat, in which you lean slightly forward of the vertical to free the horse's hindquarters for jumping (see the figure on this page). When I started dressage, one of the hardest habits for me to undo was the tendency to perch forward, which I learned in the hunt seat genre. Whenever I tried to correct this habit, I would revert to a chair seat and would then have difficulty keeping my legs under me. Essentially, I had to learn to ride all over again, retraining each body part, until the new, unfamiliar classical position eventually began to feel natural to me. So if you take up dressage from another discipline, be prepared to go back to the basics at the Introductory Level and work your way up, no matter how many years you've been riding.

This rider is demonstrating the forward seat on her stationary horse. Note how her seat is out of the saddle (for jumping) and, therefore, cannot influence the horse's hindquarters until she sits back down.

Starting over is a truly humbling experience, but now that I realize how much the classical principles have helped me improve my riding, I cannot imagine riding a horse any other way. The results are well worth the extra effort. I wish that I had been taught to ride this way initially, but dressage instruction simply wasn't prevalent in my region at the time. Even if I moved on to another discipline, I would still employ the classical principles I have learned, which, of course, all the best riders do. Besides, I could never again in this lifetime lean forward without hearing in my mind my instructor's voice, who with great patience constantly reminded me to "sit back!"

Cross Training

Eventers cross disciplines and pursue cross-country, stadium jumping, and dressage. Eventing is also called cross training. Experienced riders can and do switch back and forth from the jumping position to the classical seat with relative ease, and their classical training can greatly enhance their flat work on the jump course. In fact, once you know what to look for, you'll see some top-show jumping riders revert to the deeper, classical seat between jumps to steady and collect their horses for the next massive obstacle.

The Back and Abdominal Muscles

The more refined seat aids involve using the lower back and abdominal muscles to influence the horse. Individual riders learn to use these muscles in a slightly different way because of anatomical variations in the human form. But generally speaking, small, tightening actions of the buttocks and lower back muscles increase pressure on the seat bones by tilting the pelvis slightly backward. This is sometimes called bracing the back. The horse, being sensitive enough to feel this through layers of saddle leather, reacts to the pressure change by activating his hind legs more. The abdominal muscles work in concert with the back muscles to help stabilize and support the pelvis and spine.

Depending on the muscles and combination of aids used, increasing pressure on the seat bones is effective for driving the horse forward into extensions. It can also have a restraining effect as in collection and downward transitions. Beware, however, of leaning too far back, as shown in the figure on this page.

The Whip

The long dressage whip is an auxiliary aid used to reinforce the rider's leg aids. The rider holds the whip in one hand, allowing the shaft to rest against his thigh and with the tip pointing back toward the horse's haunch. The rider generally carries the whip to the inside or on the side where he needs it most. To correctly change sides, the rider flips the whip upward and over the horse's neck. If a whip is permitted in a dressage test, the rider may carry it on the side where he needs it most and is not required to switch with each change of direction.

Many people misunderstand the purpose of the riding whip and perceive its use as cruel. Although it can be misused in the

Some riders overcompensate by leaning too far back, as this rider tries to demonstrate. Note how the rein contact is too long, and the leg, spine, head, and shoulders are no longer aligned.

wrong hands, the whip is not intended to be carried as an instrument of punishment, but as a way to gently demand the horse's obedience and fine-tune his responses to the natural aids. The sensitive horse can feel and respond readily to the lightest tickle of the lash at the end of the whip. Therefore, this artificial aid generally does not need to be applied with much force.

Suppose, for example, that the rider applies a leg aid to ask the horse to step sideways. If the horse is inattentive or sluggish to respond, the rider can, with a flick of the wrist, and without removing his hands from the reins, tap the horse lightly behind his leg to reinforce his request. The result, one hopes, is a more active effort from the horse to step sideways, away from the touch of the whip.

Likewise, if the horse tends to plod along at the walk, the rider can gently tap, tap, tap the horse's haunch with the whip in rhythm with his stride to encourage the animal to move forward more freely. The walk must always appear purposeful, as if horse and rider are going somewhere.

During his early training, the horse must get acquainted with the whip in such a way that he will not fear it or tense up when the rider carries one. This is accomplished by running the whip over the horse's body and gently tapping him with it until he becomes accustomed to its touch. This is true of both the riding whip and the much longer longe whip used in ground training. A horse conditioned in this way will respond to the whip's aid without overreacting or expressing undue fear.

In 2004, the rules about the length of whips carried in recognized dressage competitions changed. Competitors may carry one whip in dressage classes (except championships) and the warm-up area. The whip may be no longer than 43.3 inches long (110 centimeters), including the lash.

Because any competition rule is subject to change, make sure you read and familiarize yourself with the most up-to-date U.S. Equestrian Federation (USEF) *Rule Book* before entering the arena. Ignorance of the dressage competition rules can cost you points in a test or even get you disqualified. Rule changes are posted on the USEF Web site at www.usef.org.

Spurs

Spurs add greater refinement to the leg aids and can make a dull, lazy horse more alert and attentive to them. However, spurs should be used only by the more advanced rider who has learned to control the position and use of his legs and seat. On the boots of a novice, whose legs may inadvertently grip or flop about at the wrong moment, spurs are abusive and likely to cause the horse to buck.

For competition, blunt metal spurs can have a curved or straight shank. If the shank is curved, it must be worn pointing downward.

Again, spurs are much misunderstood and maligned by those who don't understand their delicate application. As with the whip, spurs can be used in an abusive fashion on the wrong heels; however, equipment checks at dressage competitions are designed to spot inappropriateness.

Your Voice

The voice is an excellent training tool, and most horses readily learn to recognize and respond to the words *walk*, *trot*, *canter*, and *whoa*. However, you are not allowed to use voice commands during a dressage test, because all communication between horse and rider must be accomplished through the silent aids and nearly invisible. Still, the voice is a valuable schooling aid and useful in everyday handling. The horse understands that quiet, soothing tones mean you are pleased with him, and that sharp, growling tones mean he has done something wrong.

The most important word in any horse's vocabulary, and the first one you should teach him, is either *whoa* or *halt*. Select one or the other and use the same word consistently when you want the horse to stop. Do not confuse the horse by switching back and forth between different words that have the same meaning.

Also, if *whoa* is your halt command, choose another word besides *no* to say when the horse is being naughty. Even a sharp *no* sounds too much like *whoa* and may confuse the horse. So pick something like "Quit it" for reprimands.

In an emergency, voice commands can give you an extra edge of control while astride or from the ground. One time, I left my Quarter Horse gelding tied to an open-ended hitching post that had a bee's nest hidden inside. Gordon always loved to scratch his face against something, but when he rubbed this particular post, he rattled the bees inside and set them a-buzz. Naturally, he panicked when they started stinging. He broke free of his halter and headed for the barn at a dead gallop. When I saw him running, I yelled, "Whoa!" To my great relief (and amazement), he skidded to a halt on command and allowed me to rescue him from the remaining bees still clinging to his neck. That was the first time I truly appreciated the power of voice commands. I also was more careful about where I tied my horse the next time.

Dressage Training Principles

Horses aren't born knowing what the aids mean. They have to be taught. When starting out a youngster, a trainer must use stronger, more exaggerated aids to elicit the desired response. But with repetition and time, the horse catches on, and the aids can become lighter and more refined.

It seems obvious that a student rider who is trying to learn the aids must learn them on a horse that has been properly trained to understand and respond to them. But it's amazing how many people think they can go out and buy a green (untrained) horse real cheap and ride it, when the horse doesn't know anything. Not only is this foolish, it's extraordinarily dangerous to match an untrained rider with an untrained horse. The rider must first learn on a trained horse. Only after he has acquired a high degree of proficiency in his craft should he even consider getting on an unschooled or partially schooled horse. In all disciplines, an untrained rider must be paired with an experienced school horse, and an untrained horse must be paired with an experienced rider or trainer.

Because dressage is a system for teaching and preparing the horse (and rider) to perform movements that become more difficult at each stage, the training must follow a logical progression that conditions the horse incrementally, both physically and mentally. This is why dressage training is divided into levels, each building on the exercises of the one before. In competition, the level refers to the horse's stage of training (not the rider's), and the horse typically schools at home at a higher level but performs one level lower at shows.

Training Objectives

Dressage training aims to make the horse more supple, flexible, calm, confident, and obedient—an overall pleasure to ride. The horse's achievement of each of these qualities is expressed by:

- The regularity and free-flowing forward rhythm of his gaits
- The apparent ease with which he carries his rider and performs the movements
- The lightness and easy mobility of his forehand, coupled with harmonious engagement from the hindquarters, which creates impulsion, or pushing power
- Obedience and acceptance of the bit, without showing tension or resistance

The Training Pyramid

Modern-day dressage training levels generally follow an accepted training scale, or pyramid of training, developed long ago by equitation masters. At the pyramid's base, the trainer begins with instilling overall good manners in the horse while being handled on the ground. This is followed by introducing the horse to saddle and bridle and to having a rider on his back.

From there, the trainer proceeds up the scale to teach the horse to move forward freely and to develop rhythm and regularity in the gaits. As the horse learns to respond properly to the rider's aids, he should begin to move in a more relaxed, confident manner, accepting contact with the rider's hands through the bit without pulling or resisting. As the horse progresses in training, greater impulsion, or pushing power from behind, develops, along with improved straightness and ability to bend around the rider's leg.

Finally, at the top of the scale, collection develops. *Collection* is a state in which the horse is gathered together. The collected horse holds himself in a shorter frame than, say, a horse in Training Level. That is, the collected horse's outline is shorter from nose to tail, the neck is arched gracefully and, depending on the pace, his strides are shorter and higher.

In gathering himself, the horse gradually engages his hindquarters, moving them closer to the forehand, thus elevating the forehand to produce a feeling of lightness and easy mobility in the rider's hands. Once experienced, this elusive feeling of lightness remains with a rider for a lifetime. Difficult to describe in words, the quality of lightness is that sense of being "one" with your horse, as if all you need to do is think the next movement and the horse reads your thoughts and responds accordingly. It is the epitome of harmonious communication between two species, a prize to strive for during every ride, and an exhilarating, natural high like no other. For many of us, the pursuit of lightness is what fuels our addiction for the sport and art of dressage.

Overview of the Gaits

A gait is a manner of moving on foot. The basic gaits or paces of the dressage horse are the walk, trot, and canter. These gaits are natural to all horses, but some are more gifted movers for dressage than others. Most notably, the warmblood breeds, such as the Hanoverians, Holsteiners, Westphalians, Trakehners, the Selle Francaise, and the Swedish, Dutch, and Belgian Warmbloods, have been specifically bred for the elastic paces and balanced conformation (body build) necessary to excel in competitive dressage. With careful, thoughtful training, any horse's "way of going" can be polished and refined for improved performance in the show ring, but not all can achieve the higher levels of dressage.

A change from one gait to another is called a transition. Transitions are not merely slowing down and speeding up, but a change in the movement or gait. For example, striking off at the trot from a walk is an upward transition; the change from canter back to trot is a downward transition. In a dressage test, transitions must occur smoothly and precisely at the designated marker, with no abruptness or resistance.

The Walk

Of all the gaits, the walk is perhaps the most neglected, as most beginners underestimate its importance in the dressage tests. A good walk in dressage is never ambling, but always energetic and "going somewhere," as if on the verge of breaking into a trot. A lazy walk will cost you points.

Simply speaking, alternating leg aids against the horse's sides cue him to walk. The walk has four beats as each foot strikes the ground separately in marching fashion. The sequence of footfalls is near hind, near fore, off hind, off fore. (In horsemen's lingo, the left side of the horse is called the near side, because it's the side on which the rider mounts; the off side is the right.) Training refines the walk into several distinct variations: the collected walk, the medium walk, the extended walk, and the free walk.

Collected, Medium, and Extended Walk

The collected walk is shorter than the medium walk and more elevated with higher steps. The medium walk shows moderate lengthening, with the hind feet stepping well under and touching the ground in front of the footprints of the forefeet. The extended walk is long and deliberate, like the medium walk, but the horse covers more ground as he is allowed to stretch out his head and neck on contact.

Free Walk

The free walk, as the name implies, is a reward and relaxation pace for the horse in which he is given a loose rein and allowed to stretch down freely. Although the horse is permitted to relax, the rider must still keep his mount purposefully moving forward in the free walk and not allow the gait to deteriorate to an aimless shuffle.

Newcomers to the sport of dressage sometimes ask why the horse is allowed to free walk in the middle of a dressage test. The reason is the judge wants to see how calmly and precisely horse and rider can gather themselves together from a relaxed pace and move back into a working gait. Doing so is not as easy as it looks. In fact, nothing in dressage is as easy as it looks, but good riders and well-trained horses can make it look that way, which is part of the art.

The Trot

To signal the horse to strike off into a trot, the rider pushes forward with his seat and squeezes both legs against the horse's sides at the same time. A trotting horse taps out a distinct, two-beat gait as alternating diagonal pairs of legs, near hind and off fore followed by off hind and near fore, strike the ground, as shown in the figure on this page. A moment of suspension, during which all four feet are briefly off the ground, occurs as one diagonal pair of legs leaves the ground and the other pair lands.

In the trot, you can clearly see how the alternating diagonal pairs of legs, near hind and off fore followed by off hind and near fore, strike the ground.

Rising Trot

The rider either sits the trot or rises on an alternating diagonal pair of legs. Rising to the trot is called posting. The rider is said to be posting on the right diagonal if he rises slightly out of the saddle as the right front leg or shoulder comes forward. Then, as the left foreleg comes forward, the rider sits softly back in the saddle, without bouncing Similarly, if the rider rises with the left front leg or shoulder coming forward, he is said to be posting on the left diagonal.

To an onlooker, posting looks like the rider is simply bouncing up and down in the saddle in rhythm with each diagonal stride. The correct motion is soft and controlled and involves tilting the pelvis forward from the hip joints, then settling back in the saddle. Many beginning riders mistakenly rise at the trot by pushing up with the thigh muscles or knees, or pushing off from the stirrups. Either of these inhibits their ability to apply effective leg aids at this gait and makes the exercise much harder work than it needs to be.

Most riders are taught to post on the right diagonal when the horse trots around the arena with his right side to the fence, or to the outside of the arena. Likewise, the rider posts on the left diagonal when the horse's left side is to the outside. The primary purpose in switching diagonals is to help ensure that the horse develops his muscles evenly on both sides. Switching is accomplished easily by simply sitting for a beat, then rising on the new diagonal. With practice, switching diagonals at each change of direction becomes second nature to a rider, and the rider learns to feel when he is posting on the wrong diagonal.

All horses favor going to one side or the other, much like people who are either right-handed or left-handed. Because of this, posting on a young or green horse's favored side usually feels more comfortable to the rider. However, if the rider posts only on the favored side all the time, the horse bears the rider's full weight in the saddle only on that one side, which eventually can cause that side to become stronger than the other side. Careful, even work going in both directions helps to develop an evenly muscled, more balanced horse, which is essential in dressage.

Sitting Trot

Sitting the trot is a lot more difficult for some dressage riders to learn than posting. Sitting trot also is generally less comfortable to the rider at first, at least until training progresses to the point where he can gather and maintain his horse in a more rounded, collected frame. That sitting the trot can be so difficult often comes as a great surprise to some riders who transfer to the sport from other equestrian disciplines. After all, the sitting trot looks much easier than posting, and the cowboys on their western horses make it look so relaxing.

Certainly, sitting the trot is easier on some horses that have flat gaits with little hock action. But this is not the case at all on a big-moving warmblood capable of nice impulsion from the hindquarters. That thrust from the rear end adds quite a bit of spring to the gait, which takes some getting used to for the rider who's never sat a horse trained in dressage gaits before. But mastery of the sitting trot is imperative in this sport, as dressage tests call for all trot work to be done sitting, except at the novice levels.

Working versus Collected Trot

Dressage tests also call for working trot, collected trot, medium trot, and extended trot. Working trot is a balanced, freely forward moving, active pace, a good choice for the horse not yet fully trained and ready for the collected trot. In collected trot, the horse moves with shorter steps, with neck raised and arched, and with hocks well engaged, pushing energetically from behind.

Extended Trot

Medium trot falls somewhere between working trot and extended trot, allowing moderate lengthening. A well-executed extended trot shows maximum lengthening, covering as much ground as possible, with forelegs and hind legs similar in their forward degree of extension. It is often executed across the arena on the diagonal line (see the figure on the next page) and is always a crowd pleaser when performed by a horse blessed with spectacular gaits.

In a good, ground-covering extended trot, the diagonal fore and hind legs should be parallel in their degree of extension.

Collected and extended trot are refined show ring gaits seldom seen in everyday hacking.

Passage and Piaffe

Two other greatly refined forms of the trot are seen in dressage: the passage and the piaffe. Because they are attempted only after the horse graduates to the higher levels of dressage, they are sometimes referred to as high school (*haute ecole* in French) movements.

The passage (like dressage, it rhymes with *massage*) is a cadenced, elevated (collected) trot with a touch of prolonged suspension as each alternating diagonal pairs of legs strike the ground. The piaffe is a cadenced, elevated passage in place, sometimes called trot on the spot. It is the most difficult form of the trot, requiring maximum collection and impulsion for a one-ton animal to move energetically in place without advancing forward, and look graceful and beautiful while doing it.

The Canter

Sometimes described as a slow gallop, the canter is a three-beat gait, in which three hoofbeats can be heard for each stride. As with the trot, dressage tests recognize the working canter, the collected canter, the medium canter, and the extended canter. These call for similar demonstrations of collection and lengthening at the canter.

The gait is distinguished as leading right or leading left. In right lead canter, the horse lifts the left hind leg first, followed by a power push from the left fore and right hind diagonal, and finally the right fore, followed by a moment of suspension with all four feet in the air before the next stride commences. For the left canter lead, the sequence of footfalls is reversed. In the right canter, the right foreleg and right hind leg "lead" or reach farther forward at their point in the stride than the other legs, as shown

In the canter, one pair of lateral legs reaches further forward than the others. This is known as the leading leg. In the right lead canter, the right foreleg and hind leg reach further forward. In left lead canter, it is the opposite.

in the figure on the previous page. In left canter, the left lateral pair lead in the same way.

The Aids for the Canter

To signal the horse to canter on the right lead, the rider presses his right leg strongly against the horse's side at the girth, while simultaneously swinging his left leg back to touch the horse behind the girth and pushing forward with the seat. In dressage, the rider keeps his aids on the horse in this manner throughout the canter. For left canter, the aids are reversed.

The mechanics of the aids are simple in theory: When the rider swings his left leg back to touch the horse behind the girth, the horse reacts to this slight pressure by picking up his left hind leg. This sets up the proper footfall sequence for the right lead canter, the power push from the left fore and right hind diagonal. The rider's right leg at the girth acts as the driving aid, telling the horse to reach further forward with his right hind leg under him. The rider also drives with his seat, not bouncing, but allowing his seat to slide back and forth in the saddle with the horse's motion, as if polishing the leather.

Change of Lead

Cantering on the correct lead in a given direction helps the horse balance himself better at turns and corners, because the leading hind leg comes further under his body for that pivotal support. Most horses favor one lead over the other, usually the left, and are easier to ride at canter on the favored lead. Generally, the rider asks the horse to change leads at each change of direction. This may be accomplished with a change of lead through the trot, a simple change, or a flying change. In change of lead through the trot, the rider brings the horse down to a few strides of trot, and then asks the horse to strike off at the canter on the new lead. In the simple change, the rider brings the horse down to a few steps of walk, then restarts the canter on the opposite lead with no trot steps in between.

Flying and Tempi Changes

The more difficult flying changes occur "in the air," in conjunction with that moment of suspension before the next canter stride commences. Flying changes are executed at the canter whenever a change of direction is required. The rider must learn to feel the right moment within the stride to signal the horse for the change and coordinate his aids precisely.

In the higher levels, flying changes are also executed in a series, called tempi changes, at every fourth, third, or second stride, or at every single stride. Spectators can more easily see these flying changes when they are executed in a series down a straight line. Single tempis are especially good crowd pleasers, particularly when performed to music, as the horse appears to be skipping or dancing to the beat.

Counter-Canter

There is also a special balancing movement in dressage called the counter-canter, in which the rider deliberately asks the horse to canter on the "wrong" lead. For example, on a circle to the right, the horse is asked to canter on the left lead. The cues given to the horse are the same for the left lead canter, but instead of circling to the left, he's asked to circle to the right. Counter-canter is preparatory to developing the straightness, suppleness, and balance required of the horse to execute tempi changes and other advanced movements. Many riders find the counter-canter especially difficult to master, because it demands precise awareness, coordination, and control of the aids and body position, qualities that are essential before moving on to upper level work.

Overview of the Levels

As mentioned, dressage training progresses in levels. Each level has four dressage tests, which are used to determine whether horse and rider are ready to move up to the next level. The lower-level tests (through Fourth) are designed by committees from the USEF and the U.S. Dressage Federation (USDF) and are revised every four years to allow for improvements in competition. The upper-level tests (Prix St. Georges, Intermediate I and II, and Grand Prix) are written by the Federation Equestre Internationale (FEI) and are the same worldwide, regardless of where they are performed. These tests are also revised periodically on a staggered schedule.

Introductory Level

As the name implies, this level is a preparatory stage that allows the horse and/or rider new to dressage to demonstrate elementary skills while getting acquainted with dressage show protocols. At this level, the horse must accept the rider's cues and move forward obediently. Simple patterns are performed at walk and trot, with importance placed on how well the rider prepares the horse for each movement. Also at this early stage, the rider is permitted to post or rise at the trot, whereas, as he progresses up the levels all trot work must be sitting, unless otherwise indicated. No canter work is required in Introductory Level tests, which can be viewed or ordered online at www.usdf.org.

Keeping in mind that all dressage tests are periodically revised, there are currently two tests, designed by the USDF, at this level:

- **Introductory Level Test A:** Includes working trot rising, medium walk, twenty-meter circles at the trot, free walk, and halt through the walk.
- **Introductory Level Test B:** Similar in content to Test A with the addition of a change of rein at the trot. A change of rein is a change of direction accomplished in this case by crossing the arena on the diagonal line from the corner letter F through X at the center to the opposite corner letter H. At X, the rider sits a beat to change the diagonal on which he is posting.

Training Level

This level is widely viewed as the first category for novices at recognized U.S. dressage shows. Building on the basics learned in

Introductory Level, Training Level requires the horse to demonstrate suppleness and the ability to move forward freely with a clear, steady rhythm, while willfully accepting contact with the rider's hands through the bit and reins. Canter work is added, with emphasis on smooth departs and transitions through the trot.

The national-level tests, Training through Level 4, can be viewed or ordered online at www.usef.org. There are currently four Training Level tests:

- **Training Level Test 1:** Includes working trot, working canter, medium walk, free walk, twenty-meter circles at trot and canter, and halt through the walk. Trot work at Training Level can be sitting or rising, unless stated.
- **Training Level Test 2:** Builds on Test 1 with directional changes and variations that make the movements somewhat more challenging.
- **Training Level Test 3:** Builds on Tests 1 and 2, adding half-circles and the stretch circle at the trot. The twenty-meter stretch circle allows the horse to stretch his neck forward and downward. The rider must continue to keep the horse moving forward without any change in the rhythm of the pace, even as he shortens the reins and takes the horse back.
- **Training Level 4:** Builds on the previous tests, adding the one loop, in which the rider trots off the rail from the corner, tracks across the diagonal, changes direction and bend at X (see the figure on the next page), and moves back toward the rail on the diagonal.

First Level

Besides all Training Level requirements, horses showing at First Level must demonstrate improved balance, impulsion, and throughness. *Impulsion* is the thrust or pushing power from the hindquarters, and it is the foundation for all future dressage

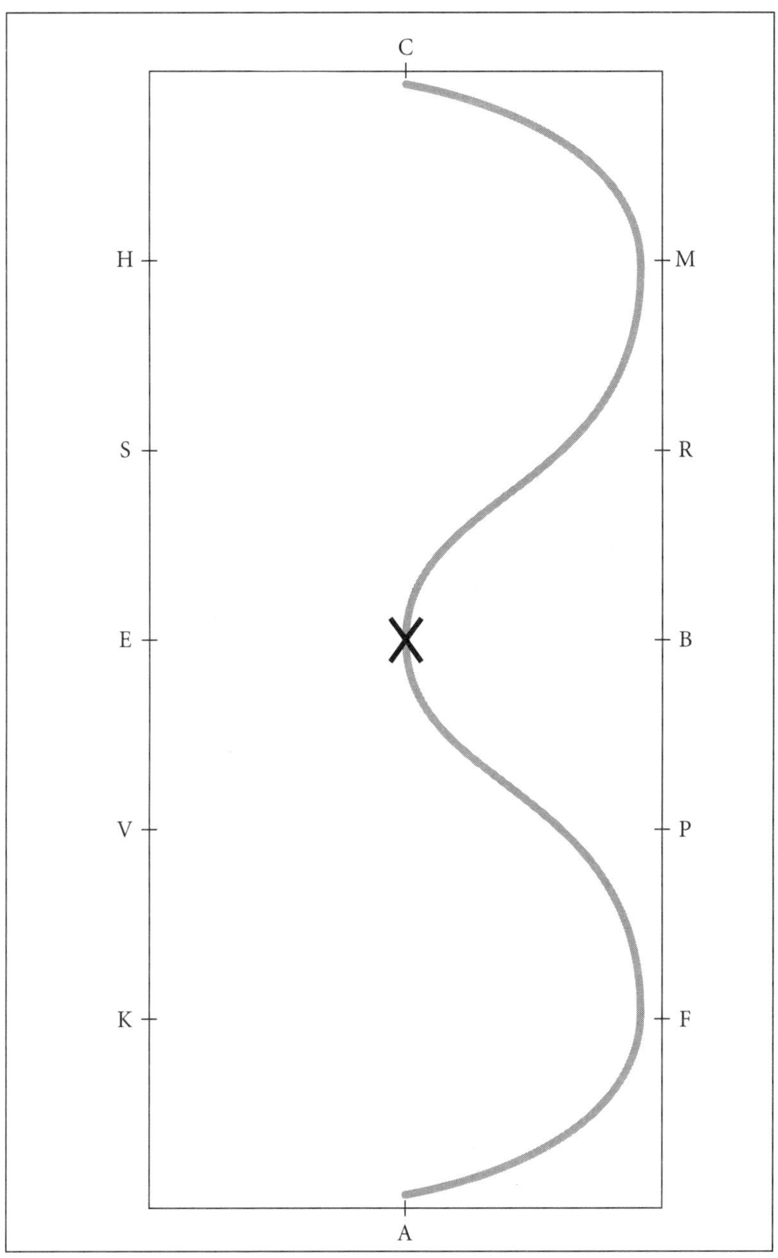

The one loop demonstrates a change of bend at X.

work. The horse's engine is in the back end, so to speak, and that power coming from behind with active haunches is the energy source that propels the forward motion.

The more elusive quality of throughness is a soft, supple connection to the rider's aids that allows the energy of the movement to flow freely through the horse's body from hindquarters to bit and back again. First Level also requires the horse to leg-yield, a side-pass maneuver in which the horse moves away from the rider's leg aid, stepping well under with the hindquarters and crossing the legs over in the direction it is going. This movement is the basis for future lateral work. Elements emphasized in First Level improve self-carriage, preparing the horse for the collected and medium gaits required at Second Level.

There are four tests at this level:

- **First Level Test 1:** Builds on and refines the requirements of previous Training Level work, adding the three-loop serpentine (as shown in the figure on the next page), lengthening of stride at the trot, a ten-meter half-circle at the trot, a fifteen-meter circle at canter, and more challenging directional changes.
- **First Level Test 2:** Introduces leg-yielding at the trot and lengthening the stride at the canter.
- **First Level Test 3:** Introduces change of canter lead through the trot.
- **First Level Test 4:** Introduces the counter-canter.

Second Level

The true dressage gaits begin here with all work showing a greater degree of suppleness, straightness, throughness, and balanced self-carriage. The collected gaits required at this level must show a greater degree of impulsion and engagement from the hind end and more elevation or self-carriage in front. Building on

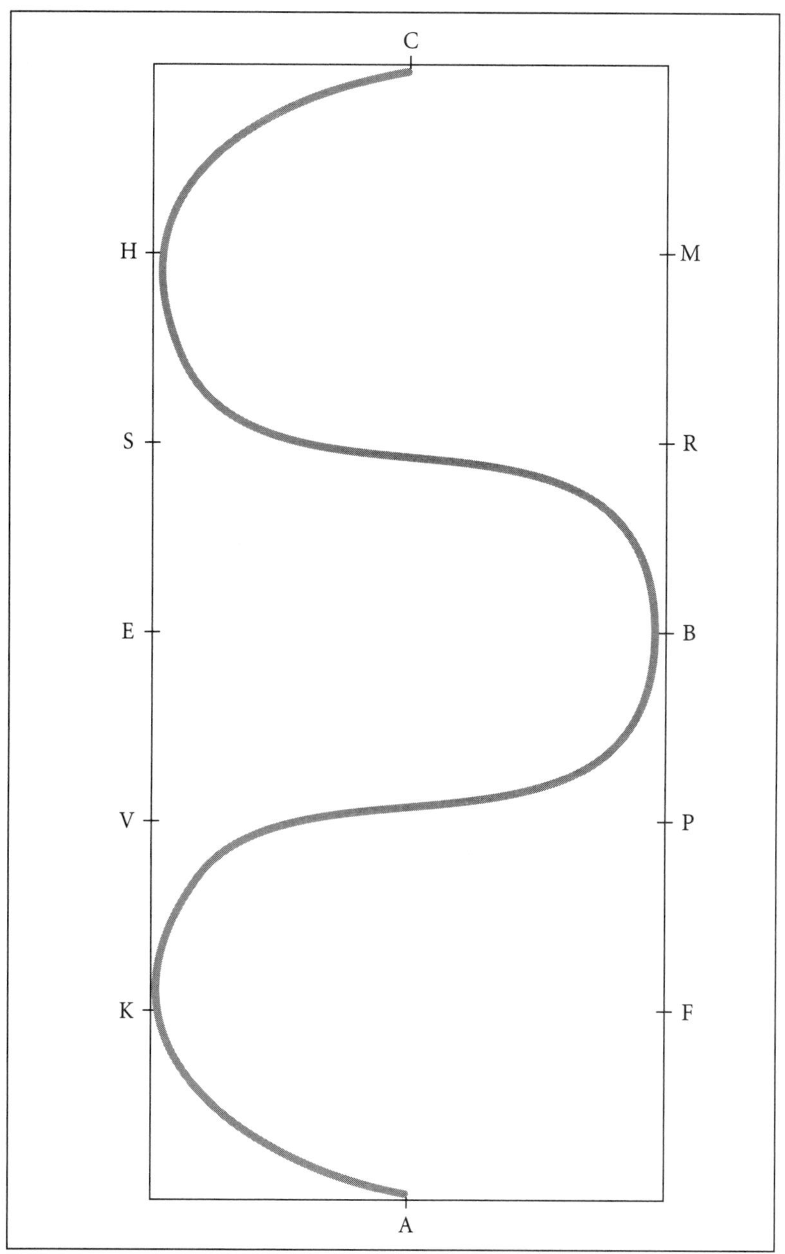

A three-loop serpentine.

leg-yielding exercises from First Level, Second Level uses the lateral movements—shoulder-in, travers, and renvers—to improve bending. Second Level also emphasizes smooth, precise, and well-prepared up and down transitions, as they are an excellent training tool for improving collection.

There are four tests at this level:

- **Second Level Test 1:** Builds on and refines all previous work, adding medium and collected gaits, the ten-meter circle at the canter, the rein-back (backing up), the shoulder-in, and simple change of lead at canter. To execute a simple change of lead, the rider brings the horse down from canter to a few steps at the walk, then restarts the canter on the opposite lead.
- **Second Level Test 2:** Introduces travers (haunches-in) and the stretch circle at the canter.
- **Second Level Test 3:** Introduces the turn on the haunches, in which the horse's forehand moves at the walk in even, regular steps around the inner hind leg.
- **Second Level Test 4:** Introduces renvers, which is the inverse of travers, with the horse's haunches aimed toward the rail instead of his head.

Third Level

Flying changes at the canter come at this stage, building on principles learned at Second Level. Lateral movements, such as the half-pass, show greater collection. The horse demonstrates a clear distinction between the collected, medium, and extended paces, showing overall improvement from Second Level work in rhythm, suppleness, straightness, collection, throughness, and impulsion. Impulsion has improved to the degree that the horse possesses greater elasticity, allowing him to lengthen or shorten his strides without losing his forward-moving fluency.

The leap from Second to Third Level is a big one, requiring three tests to prove proficiency:

- **Third Level Test 1:** Refines and builds on all previous work, introducing the extended gaits, the half-pass at the trot, and the single flying change at the canter.
- **Third Level Test 2:** Introduces the half-pass at the canter, eight-meter trot circles, and the inside rein release at the canter. The German word for a rein release is *uberstreichen.* It's a brief release of the contact, during which the rider extends his hand forward and rides off contact for several strides. Its purpose is to demonstrate that the horse can maintain self-carriage, tempo, and gait quality, even on a loose rein.
- **Third Level Test 3:** Introduces the release of both reins at the canter and the transition from rein-back to extended walk.

Fourth Level

The gymnastic exercises at the previous levels progressively condition the horse's muscles to a high degree of suppleness, enabling him to perform increasingly difficult movements and patterns with balance and beauty. Emphasis is refinement of the movements already learned, rather than introducing new ones. Tests at this level are designed to confirm horse and rider's readiness to move on to FEI levels of competition. Zigzags and quarter-pirouettes at the canter demonstrate the lightness and mobility of the forehand required for the higher levels.

There are three tests at this level:

- **Fourth Level Test 1:** Introduces the collected walk and canter and the counter-change of hand in trot. The counter-change of hand is a series of two more half-passes involving a change of direction, in a zigzag fashion. The counter-change of hand in canter comes in Test 3.
- **Fourth Level Test 2:** Introduces tempi changes (flying lead changes) every fourth stride and quarter-pirouettes in canter.

- **Fourth Level Test 3:** Refines all previous work with tempi changes every third stride and half-pirouettes in canter.

Keep in mind that the governing authorities that write the dressage tests also revise them periodically; therefore, the requirements described here are subject to change.

The FEI Levels of International Competition

The FEI is the international governing body for all Olympic equestrian games worldwide. Often, competitors refer to the FEI levels as simply the *upper levels*. The Prix St. Georges, Intermediate I and II, and Grand Prix levels represent the higher virtues of dressage training and competition. All dressage riders dream of eventually reaching these levels, which include:

- **Prix St. Georges:** As in Fourth Level, emphasis at this level is placed on greater and greater refinement of all previous work. Transitions are made more difficult, with less time to prepare for them.
- **Intermediate I:** More of the same, with increasing intensity and rapid-fire transitions, demanding great precision. New at this level are full canter pirouettes (Prix St. Georges calls for only half-pirouettes) and two-tempi changes (flying changes of lead every second stride).
- **Intermediate II:** This level represents the next big advance in a horse's training, as the classical high school dressage maneuvers are introduced. These include the passage, the piaffe, and the single-tempi changes. The latter are changes of canter lead at every stride, a beautiful movement that makes the horse appear to be dancing or skipping.

Musical Freestyle

This is not a level but an additional facet of competition in which horse and rider perform specified movements to music. When performed to classical music, freestyle (also called kur) is like a beautiful ballet on horseback, but any style of music can be selected, so long as the tempo coincides closely with the horse's gaits.

Of course, the more complex and memorable freestyle performances take place at the Grand Prix level; however, competitors can participate at all levels. Some show organizers even stage costumed freestyle events to attract spectator interest. Being a more artistic expression of dressage, freestyles appeal greatly to spectators, who can enjoy their beauty and entertainment value without having to know a lot about riding technique.

In freestyle competition, horse and rider are judged both on technical and artistic merit. Just like a regular test, the technical aspect of a freestyle is concerned with the quality and precision of the movements. The more subjective artistic aspect deals with the overall aesthetics of the performance, the choreography, the music selection, how well the horse's rhythm matches the music, and so forth.

- **Grand Prix Level:** The ultimate goal of every dressage rider, albeit one that few ever reach. This level confirms that the horse has achieved the requirements of classical training. This is also the level of performance seen in Olympic competition. Top Grand Prix riders move on to the Grand Prix Special, which demands the same movements but in more difficult sequences.

Additional Movements and Figures

The following sections describe additional movements and figures practiced in dressage.

The Dressage Arena

Before discussing the figures and exercises ridden in dressage, it is first necessary to describe the dimensions and layout of a dressage arena. There are two standard arena sizes. For international dressage tests, the arena is twenty meters wide by sixty meters long (see the figure on the next page). A shorter arena, twenty-by-forty meters, is also acceptable. Letters placed at specific points around the perimeter help indicate to the rider where to begin and end certain movements. The letters A and C mark the short sides, while X marks the middle of the arena. The exact reasoning behind the choice and placement of the letters has apparently been lost with time. Even though some intriguing explanations occasionally surface, the definitive rationale for what the letters stand for remains one of the sport's curious mysteries.

Voltes and Circles

Imagine a line running from A through X to C. This is called the center line. The quarter lines lie five meters to either side of the center line. The volte is a small circle up to ten meters in diameter, or from the long side to the center line. The term *circle* is used when the figure is larger than ten meters. A dressage test specifies the exact size of circle or volte to be ridden.

Riding circles looks easy but, like most things in dressage, is deceptively difficult. No other equestrian discipline places as much emphasis on riding circles correctly as does dressage. In fact, I've heard one uneducated onlooker describe dressage riders as "older ladies who spend their time riding in circles because they're afraid to jump." While the ranks of American dressage enthusiasts are predominantly women, many of us came to the sport from the hunter/jumper discipline. And my hunt seat flat work for one would have benefited from some basic dressage training.

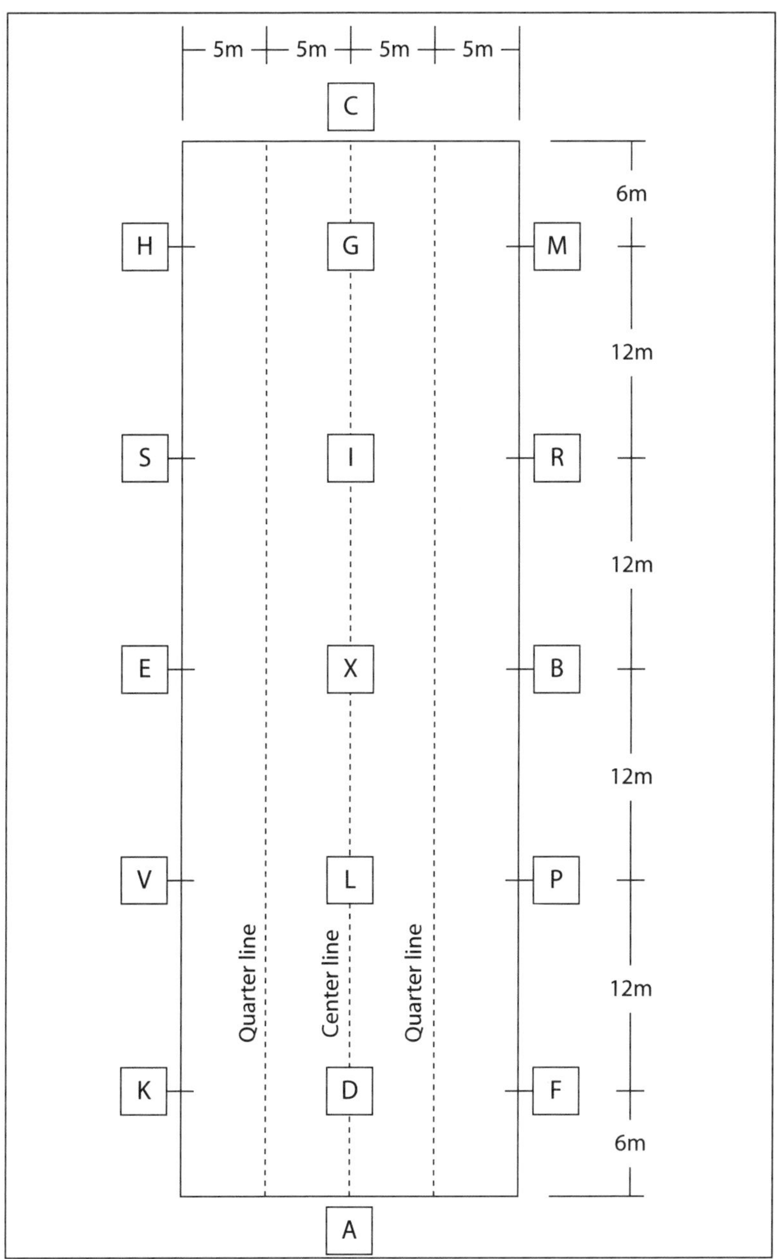

A standard dressage area is rectangular and measures twenty meters wide by sixty meters long.

Correct circles require both bend and straightness. On a curved line, as in a circle, the horse is straight if the hind feet follow the same tracks as their corresponding front feet. Neither shoulders nor hindquarters may fall in or out on the arc, and tempo must remain constant.

Figure Eights and Serpentines

The figure eight consists of two adjoining, equal-sized voltes or circles. The rider should straighten the horse an instant before the change of bend and change of direction onto the other circle.

A serpentine is a series of equal-sized half-circles that loop across the center line. The horse should be parallel to the arena's short side as he crosses the center line. Both serpentines and figure eights are excellent suppling exercises that encourage the horse to bend around the rider's leg in each direction.

The Halt

In a dressage test, you will see the rider enter the ring on his horse, halt precisely at X, and salute the judge. A good halt is square and straight, with the horse's hind legs aligned with forelegs and weight evenly distributed on all four. Front legs are parallel to each other, as are the hind. The horse remains attentive, engaged, and on the bit, in quiet contact with the rider's hands. If the horse tries to step backward, forward, or to the side or stands with one foot out in front of the others, it is considered a fault.

The Half-Halt

While not a movement that is tested in the dressage arena, the half-halt is probably the most frequently used, nearly invisible, exercise that a rider employs throughout a test or schooling session. The half-halt is a balancing tool the rider uses to prepare his horse before executing movements or transitions between gaits. It is a brief, coordinated application of the aids that momentarily increases collection, steadies the balance, and renews the horse's attention just before the new movement or transition. The rider executes a half-halt by momentarily increasing the driving effect of his seat and leg aids and regulating the forward movement from the hand, usually with little squeezes on the outside rein. The combined effect helps gather the horse by encouraging the hind legs to step more underneath his body.

Failure to use the half-halt properly results in all kinds of problems, including sloppy transitions, loss of collection, loss of impulsion, and falling out or slowing down in turns because of loss of balance. The half-halt is also a useful tool for correcting and redirecting the horse when he acts fresh or misbehaves.

The Rein-Back

This movement is more than merely backing up. The horse remains engaged and steps backward in a straight line with each diagonal pair of legs. Any resistance, anticipation, dragging, or spreading the feet or deviation from the straight line are considered faults. After completing the rein-back, the horse should be able to immediately move off into the next required pace without hesitation.

The Lateral Movements Defined

In lateral work, the horse moves forward and sideways at the same time. The lateral movements—leg-yielding, shoulder fore, shoulder-in, travers, renvers, and half-pass—help improve the horse's balance and way of going, making him more supple and encouraging him to step under his body with the hind legs and engage more.

Lateral movements are sometimes referred to as "work on two tracks" because the horse does not move straight (where the hind feet follow the same track as the forefeet), but steps with his feet on two or more tracks. Some movements can be three-track (shoulder-in) or four-track (travers).

- **Leg-yielding:** All lateral work stems from leg-yielding, a basic training exercise used to teach the horse to respond to the rider's leg aid. During the leg-yield, the

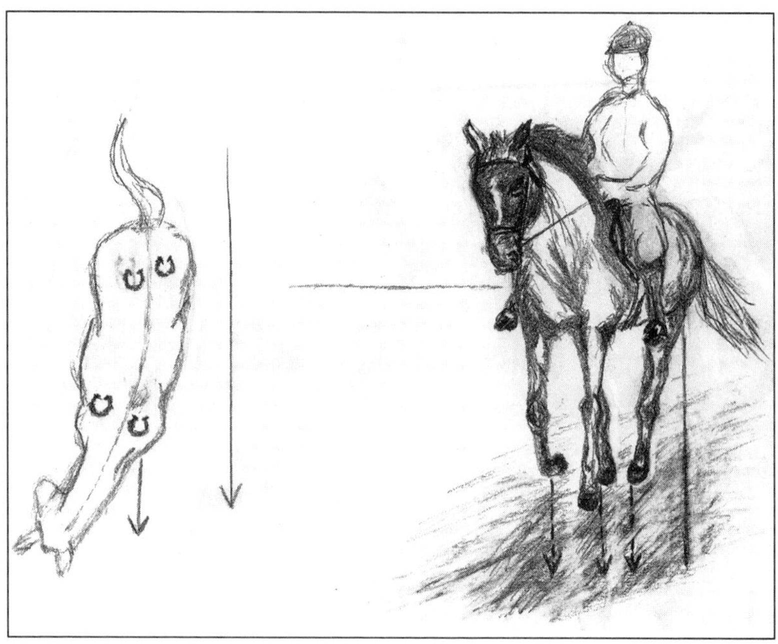

This drawing shows how the feet move on three tracks for the shoulder-in. The horse is slightly bent around the rider's leg so that he is looking at an angle away from the direction in which he is going. The movement is a good suppling exercise.

horse moves forward and sideways at the walk, trot, or canter, staying straight except for some slight flexion at the poll away from the direction in which he is moving. The inside legs cross in front of the outside legs. Common faults are excessive neck bend, not stepping sideways, and falling out through the rider's aids. The exercise is useful in teaching the novice rider how to coordinate his inside and outside aids so that the horse cannot easily evade him.

- **Shoulder fore:** This is a training exercise similar to shoulder-in, except the angle is less. The rider brings the horse's shoulders slightly off the track to the inside and holds them there while continuing to travel forward. It is a useful straightening and suppling exercise.

- **Shoulder-in:** As in shoulder fore, the rider brings the horse's shoulders off the track to the inside, but more so at a consistent angle of about 30 degrees. The horse bends around the rider's inside leg so that he is looking away from the direction in which he is moving. The horse's inside front leg crosses in front of the outside leg. The inside hind leg steps in front of the outside hind. (See the figure on the previous page for an example of shoulder-in.) By forcing the horse to step well underneath his body with the hind leg in this manner, the movement becomes an exercise in collection, as well as in suppling and straightening.
- **Travers:** Also called haunches-in, this exercise is easy to remember as the opposite of shoulder-in. The horse's

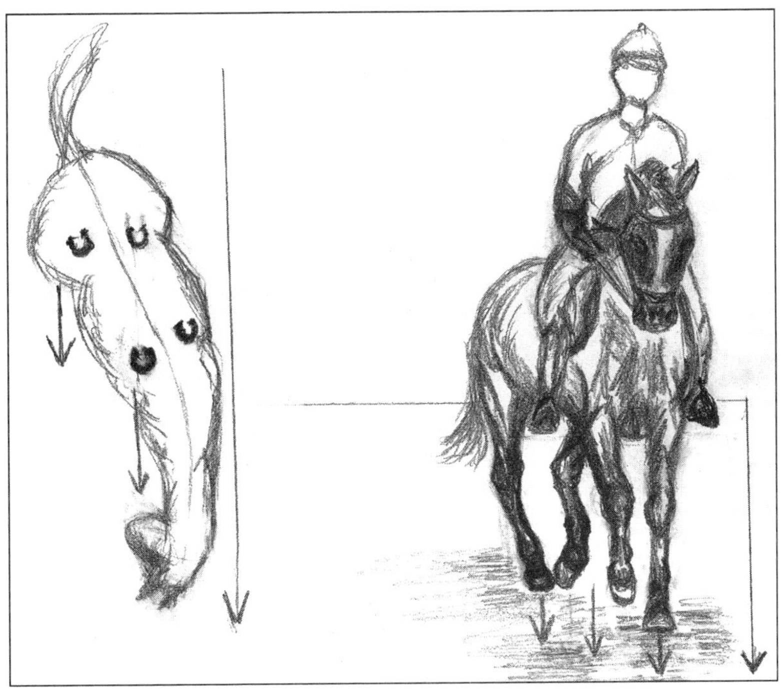

In travers, or haunches-in, the horse's outside hind leg crosses in front of the inside leg. The horse is bent around the rider's leg and is looking in the direction he is going.

shoulders remain on the track while the rider brings the hindquarters slightly off the track to the inside at an angle of about 30 degrees. The horse bends around the rider's inside leg and looks in the direction that he is moving. The horse's outside legs cross in front of the inside legs. See the figure on the previous page for an example.

- **Renvers:** This is the inverse of travers and is more difficult, with haunches to the outside and shoulders in. Unlike shoulder-in, the horse bends into the direction he is traveling. The figure on this page shows an example of renvers.
- **Half-pass:** In this variation of travers, the horse moves forward and sideways diagonally across the arena. Again, the horse bends slightly around the rider's leg and looks in the direction he is going. This is different

Renvers is the inverse of travers, with the horse's hind end instead of his head to the fence or wall. Again, the horse is bent around the rider's leg and is looking in the direction he is going.

In the half-pass, you can see the outside foreleg crossing in front of the inside foreleg as the horse moves forward and sideways at the same time.

from simple leg-yielding, in which the horse looks *away* from the direction in which he is going. In half-pass, the horse's body remains nearly parallel to the long side, although the forehand is slightly in advance of the hindquarters, as shown in the figure on this page. The outside legs cross in front of the inside legs. Performed at trot and canter, a well-executed half-pass makes the horse appear to glide effortlessly across the arena, as if dancing.

- **Counter-change of hand:** When the horse half-passes to the right, then changes direction and half-passes to the left, this is a counter-change of hand. In advanced work, the horse may zigzag diagonally across the arena first one way and then the other. The change of direction can be performed at the trot or canter. When performed at the canter, the horse must also execute a flying change of lead with each change of direction.

Chapter Three

Your Dressage Education

The Importance of Dressage Instruction

Dressage is not something you can teach yourself. Reading books and watching videos enhance the learning experience, but if you truly want to learn and benefit from classical training, take riding lessons from a qualified dressage instructor. When starting out, select someone who rides at least Third or Fourth Level, or preferably higher, not someone who simply rides and "does a little dressage." It is essential to work with a coach on the ground who is knowledgeable and accomplished enough in the classical principles to discern your aids, determine where your problems lie, and then work out solutions with you.

Later on, after you've learned the basics and begin to move up through the levels, you may need to shop for another instructor who can coach you from Fourth Level and beyond. Remember, however, you don't have to aim for the highest levels. Even basic dressage training can help enhance your riding skills and enjoyment, no matter what equestrian discipline you prefer to pursue.

Reasons for Taking Dressage Lessons

People pursue dressage for various reasons: as sport, art, or merely recreation. Some study with a dressage instructor for a short time with specific goals in mind. Others commit full time to developing their full artistic potential within the discipline. Regardless of why you choose to pursue dressage lessons, the following are just a few ways studying the discipline can ultimately benefit you as a rider:

- Provides a solid foundation of riding theory and principles
- Emphasizes proper use, coordination, and balance of the aids
- Develops proper body position through a secure, classical seat
- Builds rider confidence
- Enables the rider to deal with lazy, young, green, or problem horses more effectively
- Emphasizes riding safety
- Teaches the rider how to be an effective rider/trainer
- Teaches the rider how to ride most any horse well and improve his overall way of going
- Teaches the rider how to become a thinking rider in control of the horse's every step, rather than just a passive passenger

Signs That You Need an Instructor's Help

Nearly all riders encounter difficulties with their own horses at one time or another. Some blame the horse, but a wise horseman knows that most problems stem from some fault or shortcoming of the rider. (See the figure on the next page for an example of a rider's fault.) Often, the rider's skill level is simply not adequate enough to recognize and deal with the problem effectively. Working with a dressage coach can help improve your skills to the point where eventually you'll be better equipped to identify and resolve such problems on your own.

This rider demonstrates how improperly pointing the toes out to the side takes your lower leg contact away from the horse's sides. A rider with this fault needs help correcting her seat and position.

The following are some common riding faults that can be corrected with good, consistent riding instruction and training:

- **Fault:** The horse goes crooked, bent more to one side than another, on a straight line.

  Common cause: The rider does not properly coordinate the outside and inside aids to keep the horse straight.

- **Fault:** The horse cranks his neck to the outside of a circle or falls out through the shoulder in turns.

  Common cause: Again, the rider hasn't properly balanced his outside and inside aids to correctly bend and hold the horse straight on turns.

- **Fault:** The horse consistently fails to pick up the correct canter lead in one direction.

  Common cause: The rider is one-sided and uses conflicting aids or stronger aids on one side, resulting in a one-sided horse that strongly favors one lead.

- **Fault:** The horse carries his head too high when ridden.

  Common cause: The rider has not learned how to put the horse on the bit and use the rein aids correctly.

- **Fault:** The horse cocks his nose or neck to one side.

  Common cause: The rider is uneven in his hands or rein aids and does not have the horse properly on contact.

- **Fault:** The horse goes heavy on the forehand and leans on or pulls against the reins.

  Common cause: The rider relies too heavily on the reins for balance, instead of balancing from a correct seat and body position and using her seat to encourage the horse to step under his body with his hind legs.

- **Fault:** The horse plods along in a sluggish manner.

  Common cause: The rider does not aggressively and properly employ the driving aids to move a lazy horse forward.

- **Fault:** The horse resists, bolts, or otherwise misbehaves when the work duration or intensity increases.

  Common cause: There are, of course, many reasons for resistance and misbehavior, but often it is a result of the rider being tense or fearful; using rough, inconsistent, or conflicting aids; asking the horse to do something he is incapable of doing; or otherwise creating conflict or discomfort for the horse. Correct instruction can help a rider gain the skills and confidence necessary to deal with, and even prevent, these situations.

- **Fault:** The horse is difficult to halt, slow down, or otherwise regulate the pace at any gait.

  Common cause: The rider does not have the horse on the bit, is not in control, and is not using proper seat and leg aids to engage the horse from behind.

- **Fault:** The horse seems unresponsive or dead to the aids.

  Common cause: The rider has used ineffective and inconsistent aids for so long that the horse has simply learned to ignore them.

- **Fault:** The rider experiences increasing levels of fear, tension, anxiety, or frustration while riding.

  Common cause: The rider lacks or loses confidence because she is over-mounted and has not gained the skills needed to feel confident and effectively influence and control the horse.

The common causes listed are by no means the *only* causes of such problems. Several factors may contribute to the same problem, as every horse and rider team is influenced by individual circumstances. The point is, however, that problem riders often inadvertently create problem horses. Even a well-trained horse can pick up bad habits and gradually become "untrained" if subjected to an unskilled or sloppy rider for a period of time. Fortunately, most issues of this nature can be helped by identifying the rider's weaknesses and working with an instructor to overcome them.

If you recognize yourself or your horse in one of the aforementioned scenarios, both of you probably would benefit a great deal from classical dressage instruction at the lower levels. A good instructor can identify the causes behind your problems, help you understand what's happening and why, and work with you to resolve them.

Arranging Dressage Lessons

Dressage lessons are not cheap. You can expect to pay from at least $50 on up per hour for a private lesson, depending on where you live and what price the market will bear in your area. Group lessons are usually less expensive, but generally not as effective in this discipline. Every rider has different issues and problems, and the instructor must work with each student individually to help her improve. Most people feel the one-on-one attention of a private lesson is worth the extra investment. Ask if you can receive a discount by paying up front for a package deal of multiple lessons. Also ask whether there are any cancellation charges for missed lessons.

Most people take one hour-long lesson a week and practice riding their own horse in between. If you're financially able, invest in as many lessons as you can afford, and ride as often as you can, because you'll progress faster.

Lesson arrangements can vary, depending on the individual instructor's set up. For example, the instructor may or may not have access to school horses for students to ride at her barn. Finding a qualified instructor with an older, well-mannered, upper-level dressage horse, called a schoolmaster, for you to learn on is the ideal situation. It is far easier to learn on a well-trained horse that already knows the dressage movements.

Otherwise, you may have to haul your own horse to the instructor's place to ride during your lessons. Or you may find an instructor who is willing to travel to your home to teach you on your own horse. If your horse is also new to dressage, your progress will be slower, because you'll both be learning something new together at the same time.

Access to a riding facility with an indoor arena is a plus, because your training schedule will not be interrupted by inclement weather conditions. In many regions, outdoor riding is sporadic at best during winter. During rainy seasons, footing is often too slick and muddy for safe riding.

WHAT TO EXPECT IN THE BEGINNING

If you've never saddled a horse before, the instructor will start at the beginning and show you how to groom and tack up the mount you're going to ride. For the first two or three sessions, you can expect such ground chore instructions to be part of your regular lesson time, until the instructor is satisfied that you can perform these basic, routine tasks well enough on your own. Once you learn the procedures, the instructor may encourage you to arrive early enough to saddle and bridle the horse yourself before each lesson. Such an arrangement is in your favor because, if you're paying for an hour's lesson, you want to spend as much of that time mounted as possible. However, some barns with heavy schedules may not want students arriving too early for lessons, so be sure to clarify ahead of time what will be expected of you.

At your first lesson, you will also learn to mount your horse, as shown in the figure on this page. The instructor will also show you how to unsaddle and cool out your mount after the lesson

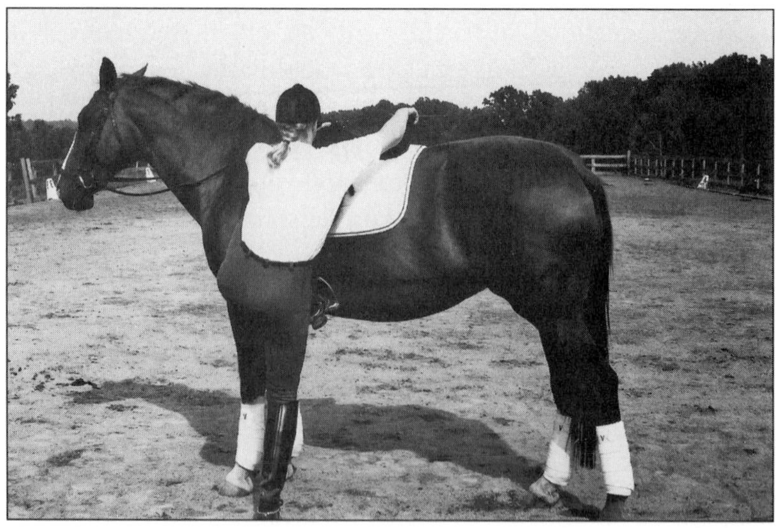

The first lesson will cover mounting, which is done from the near (left) side of the horse. This rider is neatly dressed in appropriate schooling attire.

A Word about Ground Chores

Ground chores consist of basic horsemanship skills that you must master if you plan to continue riding and perhaps own a horse someday. However, it's truly surprising how many novices expect their mounts to be ready for them when they arrive at the barn for a lesson and balk at doing any of the "dirty work." A few among the rich and famous may live this way, but after the first introductory lesson or two, the rest of us take pride in doing things ourselves. Just as skydivers pack their own parachutes, dedicated horsemen prefer to perform most tasks themselves, to ensure that the job is done to their satisfaction.

Besides, grooming, tacking up, and cooling out are activities that help you bond with the horse and develop a good working relationship from the ground. Not only that, it's important from a safety standpoint to inspect the equipment's condition before each ride, to make sure the girth is tight, to check your stirrup length, and to ensure that the bit fits in the horse's mouth correctly.

Grooming the horse beforehand helps you spot sores, dirt, or other debris that might make the horse uncomfortable enough under saddle to misbehave or perhaps unload the rider. Similarly, picking out the feet before and after riding helps ensure that a lodged stone isn't going to make your mount go lame.

Count yourself as truly fortunate if your instructor is willing to teach you other ground chores, such as mucking out stalls, braiding, clipping, or cleaning tack. There's always plenty of work around a stable, and after you learn how to do these chores, you may be able to swap a little elbow grease for free or discounted lessons from time to time.

and likely will expect you to do this chore as well, once you are comfortable with handling the horse on the ground. Altogether, you'll need to set aside approximately two to three hours of your time per lesson, not counting your drive time to and from the facility.

How Long Will You Need Lessons?

That depends on your goals and why you decided to study dressage in the first place. If you fall in love with the sport and decide you want to pursue it to the higher levels, you may spend the rest of your life honing your art. After you learn the basics and have been riding for a while, someone will inevitably ask why you're still paying for riding lessons if you already know how to ride.

Riding, like any other athletic endeavor, requires coaching to get better at the game. As long as you continue to train or compete, you'll need a coach on the ground watching what you do, because you can't see yourself ride. No matter how good you eventually become, you'll always need a pair of "educated" eyes on the ground to critique your work from time to time. Even Olympic-caliber riders work with a coach or help each other.

If you decided to take dressage lessons to correct a problem between you and your horse, or to improve your horse's way of going for another discipline, you may need only short-term training, until you accomplish your goal. Afterward, you may even opt for a periodic "tune-up," to make sure you don't lose your newfound skills. A good instructor will let you know when you're ready to move on.

How Long Will You Spend at Each Level?

The length of time it takes to move through each level varies with every horse and every rider. Everybody wants to hear a pat answer, like "a year at each level," but it's impossible to affix a surefire figure. The truth is that each person progresses at her own pace, and a lot depends on circumstances and natural ability.

For example, if you're athletically inclined and have the time and resources to ride several hours a day on many different horses, you will progress much faster than someone who rides the same horse only two or three times a week. Even so, reaching the higher levels in dressage generally requires many years of instruction and training, often a decade or more, for both horse and rider. And not everyone is capable of attaining Grand Prix level.

Many people reach a certain level and decide for various reasons not to pursue it any further. Perhaps they realize their horse isn't conformed for higher-level dressage maneuvers, and they are content with the improvements they've already made.

As for the horse's training, you cannot rush him into the higher movements too early, before he is mentally and physically able enough to perform them. A good dressage horse peaks between 12 and 16 years. Some people like to brag that their horse reached Prix St. Georges level at age 6, but this doesn't impress knowledgeable horsemen. They know a horse pushed too hard in his early years will not last well into old age, because his joints probably endured excessive stress without adequate conditioning.

The time invested in learning to ride is something that non-horse people often have difficulty comprehending. Because television and movies convey the impression that riding is easy, many people think that it can be learned in a relatively short time. Not so. You might learn enough basics in a few weeks to stay on a dead-broke mount during a not-so-challenging trail ride, but it takes years to master the finer attributes and acquire the skills and confidence to ride different horses well. The more you delve into riding, the more you realize this.

The other misconception people commonly harbor is that, if the horse is well trained enough, all the rider must do is sit aboard and "push the right buttons." The problem is, if you don't know how to push the right buttons, the horse isn't going to put forth any more effort than he has to. If you don't know how to apply the aids for tempi changes, for example, the horse isn't going to skip across the arena for you automatically just because he knows how. You have to learn how to ask him, to give the proper signals in just the right way—with the right amount of pressure, with balanced aids, and in the right sequence—plus be able to feel when a quick adjustment is needed, if you don't receive the intended response. The sensitivity and awareness required to do this with any degree of precision is what takes so long to learn. Believe me, it's a lot harder than it looks.

People often ask me, "If you've been riding a long time, why do you still take lessons?"

My stock answer is, "Because classical riding is an art form that requires more than one lifetime to learn it all."

Good riders make it look easy, but riding, and dressage in particular, is deceptively difficult to do well. To become a good rider, you need good instruction on a well-trained horse for as long as it takes to reach the goals you set for yourself. You may be satisfied with First or Second Level, or you may want to reach higher. Once you reach a certain level, you may need to make some decisions to advance further, like changing horses or instructors.

Above all, dressage is a glorious journey, a sometimes humbling growth process during which you mature as a rider, hone your horsemanship skills, learn to understand your horse really well, and appreciate the pleasure and value that other animals on this earth bring to us. Whether you pursue classical riding as a hobby, a sport, or an art form, your own personal discovery that unfolds as you learn to communicate harmoniously with another species will change and enrich your life forever.

Finding a Dressage Instructor

When I started riding in the early 1980s, dressage was still relatively new in the United States, and good dressage instructors were hard to find, unless you lived near a large metropolitan area. In my search, I encountered a few individuals who billed themselves as "basic dressage" instructors, but they were really hunter/jumper trainers teaching regular flat work. While I learned to ride and jump from these individuals, their instruction didn't incorporate the classical training that I was ultimately seeking. Eventually, however, a few qualified dressage instructors moved into my region, and I learned of their whereabouts through talking with other horse people and asking for recommendations.

Not all instructors advertise their services because they may already be booked up with longtime students and have infrequent openings for newcomers. Often, these are the best teachers, and you usually hear about them via word of mouth, as I learned of my instructors. A word-of-mouth recommendation is a riding instructor's best advertisement. But if you don't know who to ask, where do you start?

Starting with Instructor Certification

Today in the United States, any person can sell her services as a riding instructor, with no credentials required. No uniform law exists among the states requiring individuals to complete a certification program or demonstrate proficiency in their professed field of expertise before they can teach others to ride. This makes it hard to know who's a qualified instructor, and who's not, especially for someone who's new to the horse fancy in general and doesn't know what questions to ask or what to expect. The situation is different in Europe, where most countries require would-be riding coaches to complete a training program and obtain certification before they can teach.

The U.S. Dressage Federation (USDF), established in 1973 to promote and encourage a higher standard of dressage accomplishment throughout the nation, has also sought to standardize the quality of American dressage instruction through its education programs. In 1990, the USDF implemented two programs of instructor certification for the following:

- Training Level through Second Level
- Training Level through Fourth Level

Program participants study dressage history and classical theory. They must demonstrate practical horsemanship skills and knowledge of horse show judging, longeing technique, equipment use, and above all rider safety. If you log on to the Web site at www.usdf.org, you'll find USDF-certified instructors listed by region. If you don't know who to ask or where to look for an instructor in your area, this is a good place to start. Similarly, the American Riding Instructors Association (ARIA) lists instructors certified through its program at www.riding-instructor.com. Established in 1984, ARIA's certification program includes teachers of dressage as well as those in other equestrian disciplines.

Remember, however, that in this country, you are just as likely to find an instructor who hasn't completed any sort of formal certification program, but who may be just as experienced, well qualified, and suitable for your needs. There are many excellent instructors who aren't certified and listed on these Web sites simply because they don't have to be. These are the ones who have already proven their abilities in the dressage arena and made a name for themselves. Their reputation makes them sought after as trainers and coaches.

Extending Your Search

If an Internet search fails to locate any certified instructors in your area, extend your search by asking the local horse people if they know of anyone who teaches dressage. If you don't know any horse people to ask, try contacting someone who belongs to your local dressage club. The USDF Web site lists contact information for its club chapters throughout the nation, and most clubs make an effort to promote the instructors in their region.

Another good way to search for an instructor is to attend a local dressage show, talk to the riders and horse owners, and gather information. Instructors and trainers often accompany their students to shows, and you can observe their interaction on the grounds. Shows aren't always the best places to talk to trainers at length, because they're busy helping students prepare for the next class. But if you wait for a lull, you might get a chance to chat briefly and ask for a business card or phone number.

Once you have an instructor's phone number, follow up with a call and explain what you're looking for, what your goals are, and how much riding experience you have. Some instructors will not accept beginners who have no riding experience at all. Usually, this means they don't have access to school horses suitable for novices to ride. Some instructors teach only at the lower levels, while others may take only serious students at, say, Third or Fourth Level or so and help them move up. Even if an instructor can't take you on as a student, she will usually steer you in the right direction and recommend someone else to you. Investigate every lead you're offered until you find a suitable place to start.

Arranging Lessons for Children

Children can benefit from taking riding lessons, as the figure on this page shows. If you're interested in having your child start riding lessons, select someone who has experience and a good reputation for teaching children. Generally, kids can begin learning basic riding and horse handling principles at around age 5 or 6 with careful supervision, but most are not mature enough to grasp the more cerebral dressage concepts until about age 10. Some instructors will accept preteens (9 to 12 year olds), but may be reluctant to take on the risks of working with very young children.

Riding lessons are a good way for youngsters to have fun, get exercise, and learn about competition, discipline, and responsibility.

Educational organizations such as 4-H and the U.S. Pony Clubs, Inc., provide safety-conscious avenues for youth to explore and participate in equestrian activities. If your child is horse crazy and interested in learning to ride, check out a chapter in your area.

Arranging Lessons for Your Horse

For accuracy, it's worth noting that the term *instructor* generally refers to the person who teaches the rider, while *trainer* refers to the person who teaches the horse. However, horse people frequently use both terms interchangeably, as I have in the preceding text. This is because many instructors (but not all) also train horses. Since both horse and rider are athletes in equestrian sports, the term *trainer* seems appropriate when used in either case.

If you have a horse that needs some dressage training, consider a person who can provide both services to you. Horse training is expensive, but well worth it if your horse is young or green, or if you used him for a different discipline and want to switch him over to dressage. You and your mount may gain new skills together if the trainer first spends time schooling and fine-tuning your horse to consistent aids, and then teaches you how to ride him better.

Discerning Teaching Styles

If you've taken riding lessons before, you know what to expect, and you probably prefer a certain teaching style. For example, instructors who play the role of drill sergeant and yell or swear and use a lot of verbal negatives—"Don't lean forward!"—rattle my concentration and frustrate me, causing discouragement. I am much more responsive and confident with someone who speaks calmly, uses positive reinforcement and reminders, such as "Sit back!" and kindly encourages any hint of progress. I suspect that most people react similarly.

To determine whether an instructor's teaching style meshes with the way you learn best, ask if you can watch one of her lessons. Or explain that you'd like to book a trial lesson or two, then see how the initial session goes before you make up your mind about committing to more lessons.

Here are some helpful points to keep in mind when shopping for a compatible instructor:

- Choose someone who makes you feel comfortable, confident, and at ease; someone who will gently encourage you to move out of your comfort zone and try new things, but who recognizes when you're not ready.
- Choose someone who can explain riding theory and technique in a way that's understandable to you.
- Choose someone who emphasizes horse and rider safety above all and insists on proper equipment and attire, such as a safety helmet and boots with heels.
- Choose someone who demonstrates a broad knowledge of horsemanship: horse care and training, stable and pasture management, show rules and etiquette, and the care, use, and fitting of tack.
- Choose someone who has experience in showing dressage and who accompanies students to shows, *if* this is where your interest lies. Some people pursue dressage purely as an art form, and they are willing to share their knowledge but have no interest in the competition aspect. Of course, this approach is fine if you have no interest in competing. But if you want to compete, find a coach who will go to shows with you.

Appraising a Training Facility

When you're new to dressage and horses in general, it isn't easy to tell whether an instructor really understands classical principles and trains accordingly. Unfortunately, you may have to wade through a plethora of backyard riders out there who "do a little dressage" and who are willing to take your money without having any creditable classical training or experience to back up their ability. Dressage is a long and arduous pursuit, and you don't want to start out wasting time and money on instructors who really don't know what they're talking about.

Do your homework. Seek out the opinions of other dressage students and horse people regarding the local instructors and trainers in your area. If you have a friend who is knowledgeable about horses, invite her along to assess a riding facility or to watch a lesson and give you an opinion of the instructor's ability and technique.

Avoid facilities that appear to lack good management. Although stable mismanagement may not always be readily evident, certain warning signs indicate that a barn is lax in its operations. For example, avoid facilities where:

- Lessons habitually start late and then are cut short to make up for lost time
- Horses appear to be abused, underfed, neglected, overworked, or are left standing tied, tacked up, and unattended for long periods
- Smoking is allowed in the barn
- Standard safety procedures, such as wearing safety helmets and boots when mounted, are not routinely observed
- Clientele, students, and boarders don't stick around long
- Excessive tack and training gadgets are used to force a horse into a frame or certain head carriage
- Excessive debris and weeds accumulate in fields and paddocks where horses stay
- Broken fences, gates, or stalls never seem to get repaired
- Flimsy or unsafe fencing is used for horse pastures

- Stalls are not kept clean, hallways are cluttered, and the overall facility lacks good ventilation and a well-maintained appearance
- Footing in the riding arena is habitually hard, rocky, uneven, slippery, or otherwise unsafe and not well maintained

This list is by no means exhaustive, but it gives you a good idea of what to look out for when appraising a facility on your first visit.

Preparing for Your Lessons

Once you find a suitable riding facility and instructor, you'll likely be asked to sign a waiver of liability, in the event you are injured and decide to file suit later. Because we live in such a litigious society, and because novices sometimes seem unaware of how hazardous handling and riding horses can be, liability waivers have become standard procedure in most places. By reading and signing such an agreement, you acknowledge and assume the inherent risks involved in riding and handling horses. The agreement may also address fees, payment method, and the number and duration of lessons in a package deal.

Donning Safety Gear

Never forget that riding is an inherently dangerous sport. Because horses are animals of prey, they can be easily startled or frightened. Faced with a fight-or-flight situation, horses' first line of defense is nearly always to turn tail and flee from any perceived danger. Or they may rear or kick at their handlers on the ground. Although well-trained horses are taught good manners and learn to trust and obey their handlers in unsettling situations, they are still unpredictable animals and may spook or otherwise succumb to their natural instincts on occasion, whether the perceived threat is real or imagined.

Part of learning how to ride and handle horses involves acquiring the skills to maintain control and deal with situations when the horse tries to buck, shy, or bolt or otherwise misbehaves. Every rider falls off a horse at some time or another. Even experienced riders get dumped now and then, because they ride young, green, or difficult horses more often. It's part of the sport, but in most cases the types of injuries sustained are usually minor.

You can minimize the risk of serious injury by observing certain safety precautions around horses. A safety-conscious instructor will incorporate safety discussions into her lessons, teach you how to handle the horse safely on the ground, and insist that you always wear protective headgear when mounted.

Helmet

Invest in the best riding helmet you can afford, as every rider who pursues the sport long enough is destined to fall from a horse sooner or later. Safety helmets should pass or surpass American Society for Testing and Materials and Safety Equipment Institute standards for equestrian use.

One of the greatest inherent dangers during a horseback riding spill is getting stepped on or kicked in the head by the horse as you go down. Striking your head on hard ground or on a hard object, such as a fence rail, can also result in serious head trauma if the rider is unprotected. A bicycle helmet, although better than no helmet at all, is unsuitable for equestrian use because they are neither intended nor designed to withstand a kick from a horse. It's also important to realize that no helmet can protect against all injuries and that serious injury or death may still result from a horseback riding accident, even when all proper precautions are taken to minimize the risks.

Different styles of helmets are available for schooling and for the show ring. Although dressage exhibitors at any level of competition may wear protective headgear at a show without penalty, many adult competitors choose not to because they do not look as elegant as the traditional hunt cap, derby, or top hat.

Boots

When riding, always wear boots with a heel instead of sneakers, sandals, loafers, or flat shoes. In case of a spill, the boot heel may prevent your foot from slipping through a stirrup, getting your leg hung in the iron and being consequently dragged by the horse. Tall riding boots are best because they protect the inner surfaces of your legs from rubbing and chafing against the saddle and stirrup leathers; however, short paddock boots are acceptable for schooling.

Some instructors recommend and use safety stirrups, especially for beginning riders, or even for advanced riders on young, green horses. This stirrup design has an elastic band on one side that pops open to release the rider's foot in the event it gets hung in the stirrup during a fall.

Riding Pants

Riding pants are made of stretchy material for comfort and non-restricted movement. The inner legs and crotch are often reinforced for extra protection from saddle friction. Any color is acceptable for schooling lessons, but lighter colors help your instructor see your hips and seat aids better against a dark saddle.

Some people prefer to ride in blue jeans, but traditional riding breeches are far more comfortable and practical for the purpose. The stitched inseams of jeans will rub raw red lines and sores on your legs (and other sensitive areas) after enough time against the leather. Because dressage maneuvers are so difficult, riders must apply their leg and seat aids continuously to keep the horse going well in the movement. This, coupled with moving in time to the horse's rhythm, generates a fair amount of friction. Believe me, the rider isn't just sitting there trying to look pretty and elegant, and it's certainly not the horse doing *all* the work!

Shirt

For lessons, most any shirt is acceptable, even T-shirts, tank tops, or sweat shirts, as the weather dictates. However, it is preferable and more studious to wear a close-fitting, white or light-colored top,

Getting the Most out of Each Lesson

Riding lessons are expensive, so you want to make sure you get the most for your money. Here are some things you can do to help ensure that your lessons go safely and smoothly and that you gain something from each session:

- Show up early enough to get your horse ready and have the most mounted time available for learning.
- Wear proper riding attire.
- Inspect tack before mounting to make sure it's in good condition and properly fitted. Your instructor should do this, too, especially for novices, but remember that your safety is your responsibility as well.
- Check the girth before and after mounting to make sure it's tight. While being saddled, many horses suck in air and blow up their bellies, then release it after they get moving.
- Communicate your riding goals to your instructor from the outset and periodically reassess them.
- Be honest. For example, if you experience fear or trepidation when attempting something new or challenging

such as a polo shirt or long-sleeved turtleneck, neatly tucked in, so that the instructor can easily view and assess the rider's posture.

Gloves

Wear riding gloves for a better grip on the reins. Especially in hot weather, leather reins easily slip through sweaty palms and fingers, compromising your control, contact, and communication with the horse. In cold weather, insulated riding gloves help keep your hands warm without compromising feel.

on a horse, do not hesitate to tell your instructor. This is extremely common, especially for adult riders. If your instructor is aware of your feelings, she can focus on ways to help you build confidence in yourself and overcome these blocks.

- Push yourself beyond your comfort zone. For example, if riding without stirrups makes you apprehensive, make a point to drop your irons for at least a few minutes while under the watchful eyes and guidance of your instructor. With each attempt, you will gain confidence and eventually work through the issue.
- Keep a journal. After each lesson, write down what you did and what was discussed, then review it before the next lesson. You'll be amazed at how much this helps reinforce your learning.
- Ask questions if you don't understand something your instructor has covered.
- If you need a break to catch your breath, say so.
- Practice the exercises at home on your own horse between lessons.

Coat and Vest

Traditional riding coats and jackets are required in the show ring, but not during lessons. In cooler weather, wear a short, waist-length jacket or vest so that your instructor can still see your hips and seat.

Some riders choose to wear padded safety vests designed to protect the upper body and torso from excessive trauma during a fall. Protective vests are required equipment in eventing cross-country tests.

Being Fit for Riding

Many nonriders fail to understand how riding can be good exercise. Because it looks easy, they think the horse does all the work and the rider just sits there and hangs on. If their only experience with horseback riding has been a casual, guided trail ride on a dead-broke horse, then it's not hard to understand why some people may harbor this misconception. After all, these folks have never really "ridden" a horse in the true sense of the term; they've merely sat astride and been a passenger along for the ride.

The fact is, riding, particularly dressage, is a strenuous activity that demands a certain level of physical fitness on the part of both horse and rider to perform well. The progressive levels of dressage are designed to systematically condition the horse each step of the way. But if you, the rider, cannot last through an hour-long lesson of trot and canter, work without huffing and puffing and having your legs turn to jelly, that's a signal to get started right away on improving your fitness level. Ultimately, as you step up the difficulty of your riding goals, you will make better progress if your body is toned up to the task.

Success in dressage, or in any other equestrian discipline, depends on excellent muscle control, body awareness, flexibility, and stamina. Of particular importance are strong core muscles: the back and abdominal muscles that support the trunk of your body. These are the muscles that you use through your seat to engage and collect the horse. They also support and stabilize your posture to help you balance and move fluidly with the horse. If your balance is off and your posture is not properly aligned, you cannot coordinate your aids and communicate with your horse effectively. In addition, the more unbalanced you are, the harder your muscles have to work to keep you on the horse.

A regular fitness routine to maintain muscle tone and flexibility is especially important for adult riders in their 40s and older and for those who have relatively sedentary jobs and lifestyles. Lack of muscle tone and strength can predispose you to injury, fatigue, and pain.

Riding frequently, at least three times a week, will help keep you in shape, but you need to make sure you're riding correctly. For example, some people twist slightly at the waist while posting, which can lead to lower back strain and soreness. An instructor can identify such issues, which you may not even be aware of, and help you correct them.

For best results, you should supplement your riding with other cross-training activities. Out of the saddle, there are many things you can do to enhance your physical stamina and ultimately improve your performance in the saddle. Among these are walking, running, skating, weight training, aerobics, swimming, ballet, tai chi, tai bo, tai kwon do, Pilates, and yoga. Of these, my personal favorite is yoga.

Like dressage, yoga looks easy, but is deceptively difficult. It is an excellent tool for achieving unilateral strengthening and toning. Several postures, called asanas, strengthen the core muscles and help improve the support of your spine and neck. Other postures help you develop better breathing, balance, flexibility, and concentration. In time, yoga practice enhances your body awareness and refines your control of separate muscle groups. All these factors can reap great benefits in your riding.

Yoga classes are helpful, especially when you're starting out. But if you prefer solitary exercise, you can just as easily continue practicing at home on your own, using videos, yoga cards, or books.

Another of yoga's attractions is its ease of portability. You can take your mat and do it anywhere, even at a dressage show! The meditative aspects of yoga can help calm the mind, steady your show nerves, focus your concentration, and warm up those muscles for the next ride.

Chapter Four

Becoming a Thinking Rider

The Mind Game

Perhaps because horses were widely used in past centuries for transportation, many people still view them as passenger vehicles. But they aren't at all like cars or motorcycles. They are living, thinking beings with minds of their own. They did not evolve to carry humans around on their backs, so the act of being ridden is truly an unnatural state for the horse. It is only because of the horse's generous spirit and malleable nature that we are able to enter into this partnership of motion called riding.

However, horses, being conservative creatures by nature, always try to take the path of least resistance, or the easy way out. They quickly learn ways to evade their rider's aids and try to squeak by with the least amount of effort possible. This is why training and riding a horse is truly such a splendid mind game, and why many a rider has been outsmarted by his four-legged protégé from time to time.

Learning to ride well involves learning to *think* while you're riding, rather than just sitting up there and letting the horse take you around the ring. You have to analyze how your horse is going and make corrections as needed.

For example, is your horse falling out through the shoulder in turns? Is he cutting in on a circle? He is hugging too close to the fence? Is he looking off in the distance and ignoring you completely? If so, what do you, as the rider, need to do to correct him? You must think and correct quickly before small problems get out of hand. This is all part of becoming what the experts call a thinking rider.

Contrary to popular myth and misconception, you can't just sit there and expect the horse to do all the work. If you expect to sit up there on the horse's back and let him take you along for a joy ride, then you're allowing yourself to be merely a passenger who's not truly in control of the one-ton animal underneath you. Not a safe place to be. Yet, it's amazing how many people think that's all there is to riding—just sitting in the saddle and letting the horse do all the work.

Dispelling Some Riding Myths

Good riding is hard work, both mentally and physically, but good riders make it look easy and effortless. That's one reason so many people who have no experience with horses think they can just get on and ride. Or they think they can take about six weeks' worth of lessons and know all there is to know when, in fact, it takes years of experience to become a good horseman. Others harbor romanticized notions of horseback riding based on what they've seen in cowboy movies or in television ads—people galloping across the plains or riding bareback on the beach.

Then there's the common misconception that as long as the horse is properly trained, any novice can jump aboard, give a little kick to go, and just sit there and let the horse do all the work. Tourists who rent horses for guided trail rides at public parks get the idea that this is all there is to it, not understanding that they are merely passengers onboard an animal that's simply following a leader, trained to traverse the same route over and over again.

In reality, riding isn't easy at all. If it were, it wouldn't be an Olympic sport. It takes a great deal of finesse, knowledge, control, and patience to persuade a horse to go where you want him to go and do what you want him to do, especially when he would much rather be eating grass with his buddies, and especially when he decides to challenge your authority in the matter, which happens from time to time.

Dressage, in particular, is the most difficult of all the equestrian disciplines. You can't get it all in a six-week crash course. Because it is a progressive system for training the horse (and rider), it takes many years to master the nuances of classical riding (see the figures on the following page for an example of a common fault that a skilled, thinking rider can easily detect and correct). But as you learn to ride and graduate up through the dressage levels, you also learn to apply those skills to training and improving the horse.

The horse isn't the only one doing the work either, for those who can't comprehend how horseback riding is good exercise. Correct riding is a physical workout for the rider, too. It doesn't necessarily require brute strength, but it does demand great focus, concentration, balance, and body control. You use many different muscles to stay in the saddle and keep the horse going through his paces. Even a low-level dressage test can be intensely aerobic, and if both horse and rider don't break a sweat after an hour's workout, somebody isn't working hard enough.

To pursue the sport of dressage, you don't have to be a naturally gifted athlete (although it helps), but you should be in reasonably good shape to start. With regular riding, your physical condition and stamina for the sport will improve over time. People who are morbidly obese, totally out of shape, or lacking in flexibility are much more vulnerable to injury from a fall and really shouldn't take up riding until they've improved their fitness level. All serious riders adhere to some sort of exercise program, other than riding, to stay fit for their sport. Staying in good physical condition can also aid in a faster recovery, should you sustain a riding injury.

That leads us to another misconception: good riders never fall off. *They do.* In fact, every rider who rides with any frequency will fall off at some point in time. It's not a matter of *if*, but *when*, because the more often you ride, the more often you expose yourself to the possibility of a mishap. In addition, as many riders become more skilled, they tend to ride more challenging, spirited mounts or even take on the training of a green youngster, which increases the odds of a spill.

The lateral work in dressage takes time to master. This nicely executed shoulder-in shows how the movement goes on three tracks: (1) the inside foreleg, (2) the outside foreleg and inside hind leg, and (3) the outside hind leg.

Here the same horse as in the previous figure executes a shoulder-in that is on three tracks, but her nose is cocked slightly toward the fence, when she should be bent toward the inside. A thinking rider will recognize this and know how to correct it with a slight adjustment of her aids.

Fortunately, most falls do not result in serious injury. But some do, despite all safety precautions. We've all heard about riding accidents with serious or even fatal consequences. But the better rider you become, the more likely you will be able to avoid or minimize the chances of a mishap.

Another misconception that many people seem to have regarding dressage in particular is that you ride with a very light touch. The aids are applied lightly on a well-trained horse, but this is not what the term *lightness* refers to. People hear the word *lightness* used, and they think it means that you ride with little contact on the reins. This is not true. To ride a horse correctly into the bridle, you need a fair amount of contact, but not a death grip. The reins should never be slack. The rider should always be able to feel the horse's mouth, keeping an even, elastic hold on the reins.

Proper contact is achieved through driving with the legs and seat, not pulling back with the hands. You drive the horse forward into the bridle with your leg and seat aids. The horse steps under his body with his hind legs, drops his head slightly, and comes onto the bit. The neck is arched and the face is vertical or slightly in front of a vertical line drawn relative to the ground, depending on the stage of training.

On contact, you can feel the energy generated as the horse steps through the muscles of his top line—the back and neck. The energy flows in a complete circuit, starting from the horse's engine in the rear and running over the top line, through the reins to the rider and back around again. This connection is sometimes referred to as *throughness*, which is another way of saying that the horse is accepting and responsive to the aids. In this state, the horse's outline is round, not hollow in the back, and each step has some spring. A horse going in this way is much easier to control.

The roundness, energy, and eventually the collection of the more advanced horse create the sense of lightness in the bridle, so often misunderstood. But once you, as a rider, feel this glorious sensation on a horse, you never forget it, and it gives you a new understanding of what you're trying to achieve in the discipline of dressage.

The Thinking Rider versus a Joy Rider

Horses, no matter how well trained they are, sometimes respond to their surrounding environment in ways that often befuddle and frustrate their human handlers. Changes in their environment and unfamiliar sights and sounds can easily frighten and spook them. A blanket draped over a familiar fence suddenly becomes a scary object that the horse refuses to pass. An old tire tossed by the roadside could be a killer crouched in waiting. A plastic bag rustling in the breeze could signal a predator stalking in the bush, in the horse's mind.

I once owned an American Quarter Horse who was so accustomed to traffic sounds that he wouldn't flinch if a motorcycle roared past him. But if a butterfly fluttered in front of his face on the trail, he freaked out.

If you consider that horses are animals of prey and that they evolved to be constantly on the alert for predators that might eat them, it's easier to understand and cope with their ever-watchful state of alertness. Although I never figured out what kind of killer butterfly eats horses, I eventually desensitized my horse to flapping, fluttering, and flying objects by first understanding how he perceived his world, and then by using humane, thoughtful training techniques to get him accustomed to these types of objects in his environment.

As a rider, you need to know that a horse's first line of defense is always to turn tail and flee from trouble, as fast as possible. It's the old flight-or-fight reaction, and no matter how good a trainer you are, you cannot erase a survival instinct that has helped preserve a species for thousands of years. However, you can modify the behavior, as I did with my Quarter Horse, through thoughtful and knowledgeable handling. That's where the term *thinking rider* comes into the horse-and-rider partnership, because for safety's sake, the rider must be the brains, and the boss, in the relationship. Never let your guard down on a horse, and never let one take you for a joy ride, or you might end up somewhere unexpected, as in face down on the ground. You must always *ride the horse* with purpose and control, constantly out-thinking the horse's next move.

The Thinking Rider Understands the Horse's Senses

A good dressage instructor uses the term *thinking rider* a lot, because he tries to teach the student to think ahead of the horse and anticipate what the horse will do next. Part of this skill comes from understanding how the aids influence the horse. But part of it also comes from understanding how the horse uses his senses to relate to the world around him.

Eyesight

With eyes placed on both sides of their heads, horses can see almost all the way around their bodies and spot predators from hundreds of yards away. They have two blind spots that every human handler must be aware of. One is directly in front of the horse's face, the other is directly behind. For this reason, you should never approach a horse from behind without first announcing yourself. You should also never stand directly in front of a horse, in case something should startle him and cause him to bolt forward.

Each eye is wired separately into the brain in such a way that, when the horse sees something on his left side, the other side of his brain doesn't automatically perceive the same image. For instance, if a horse spooks at an object on his left, he may spook again at the same thing when you turn him around and ride past it from the right side, because he hasn't seen it from that side. If you stop the horse to let him investigate, and assure him that there's no danger, turn him toward the object, and let him view it clearly from *both* sides before proceeding.

Hearing

Horses possess a keen sense of hearing, and their ears can swivel to catch information coming from all directions. While you are riding, pay attention to your horse's ears, because they indicate where his attention is focused at the moment. If his ears are swiveling back and forth, he is canvassing his environment, but he's also being attentive to you. As his ears swivel back toward you, he is listening for your next command. If his ears are pricked steadily forward, he is alert and focused on something ahead, not you. Keep his attention and keep control.

If a horse completely flattens his ears back against his head, look out, he is expressing aggression. This is usually directed at other horses, but can be acted out against humans as well. It is a warning posture that typically precedes a kick or a bite, so always be aware of the ear position when you are working around a horse.

Smell

An acute sense of smell helps alert the horse to nearby predators on the prowl. This sense can be especially troublesome to a rider on windy days, when all manner of potentially dangerous scents may blow in from afar on a strong breeze. One whiff of something unusual, and even the most docile, obedient horse can't override the instinct to flee from a perceived danger.

Touch

Touch is one of the primary ways we humans communicate with horses, through our aids or with gentle pats on the shoulder. Their skin is so sensitive that they can feel a fly land on their back. This is important information to heed during the summer months, when biting horse flies abound. Supersensitive horses may buck when biting insects attack them. So it's wise to apply ample fly spray before you mount up.

The reason the aids work is that horses can even feel the slightest change in weight and pressure from your seat through the saddle leather and pad. Consequently, a well-trained horse can be cued with the lightest of aids that appear invisible to the onlooker.

The Thinking Rider Is a Safer Rider

By now, it should be obvious that it is much safer to be a thinking rider, fully in control, than a mere joy rider who really doesn't know much about horses, and who allows the horse to do as he pleases. An educated rider knows enough about how his horse thinks to think ahead of the horse, anticipate what's coming, adjust his aids as needed, and as a result maintain control and communication, even in difficult situations. For example, if the horse suddenly shies at an object, the rider should be able to swiftly compensate and correct, apply stronger driving aids and ride the horse past the object it fears, and continue at a normal, controlled pace. In most cases, all of this can generally be accomplished without the rider getting dumped, one hopes.

Although it's safer to be a knowledgeable, thinking rider, accidents and spills will happen from time to time, even to the most accomplished equestrians. As mentioned, the more often you ride, and the more difficult challenges you attempt, such as jumping, the more likely you are to experience a spill at some point in time. That's why safety in this sport must always be a primary consideration.

Correct riding, along with the correct training of both horse and rider, are important safety issues because they help minimize the inherent risks of horseback riding, whether you school for competition or simply want to enjoy the trails. Classical dressage *is* the correct training of both horse and rider, and the skills you acquire can help you become not only a thinking rider but also a safer rider. Even if you've been riding for a long time, dressage lessons can help improve your all-around riding skills and, as a result, enhance your enjoyment of your horse.

The Thinking Rider As Trainer

When I began taking dressage lessons, I already knew how to ride, or so I thought. I had been riding for more than a decade, first in the saddleseat (gaited horses) discipline and later in the hunt seat (jumping horses) discipline. But after my first dressage lesson, my new instructor said, "Someone taught you how to ride well enough, but he didn't teach you how to *think*."

She then proceeded to explain what she meant. For me, it was the first time I heard the term *thinking rider* used in the context of riders who can effectively troubleshoot and train their own horses. At the time, I thought I understood what she meant, but a couple more years of hard work in the saddle would pass before I could truly comprehend and appreciate the deeper meaning of her words.

She was absolutely right. Starting out in dressage, I considered myself a reasonably experienced horseman because I could walk, trot, canter, gallop, and ride circles, serpentines, and negotiate a relatively simple jump course. But the truth was my skills were such that I could neither adequately maintain nor improve my own horse's level of training.

At the time, I didn't see this as a serious shortcoming, because I never aspired to be a trainer anyway. I only wanted to ride well, and I figured that if my horse needed a training tune-up, I would simply hire a professional. But what I came to realize very soon after that first dressage lesson is that the rider *is* the trainer, and dressage (remember, it's derived from the French word meaning *to train*) systematically teaches you to be both.

Every time you ride, you're also training your horse, for better or for worse. You're teaching him either good or bad habits, depending on how correct your own riding habits are. Whenever you allow your horse to do something he shouldn't, you're teaching him that it's okay. Soon enough, a minor transgression can become a nasty habit that's hard to break.

What many people fail to understand—and what I, too, didn't realize until after I'd spoiled a couple of horses—is that a trained horse can quickly become an untrained horse in the hands of an unskilled or thoughtless rider. The degradation usually occurs gradually, as the horse learns he can take advantage of his rider's inattentiveness and evade the task required of him. If the rider's aids are unbalanced and ineffective, the trained horse stops listening and gradually becomes less responsive. Then the rider typically resorts to using stronger and stronger aids just to get the horse's attention. If the aids become abusive, whether from intent, carelessness, or simply lack of skill, the horse may rebel or resort to bad behaviors that could be potentially dangerous.

Fortunately, the first horse I acquired when I started riding possessed a fairly forgiving nature and did not rebel against aids that, I realize now after years of classical instruction, must have been unbalanced and often conflicting and confusing to the poor beast. She was a perfect horse for a beginner, gentle and unflappable, and an ideal mount for trail and pleasure riding. For many people interested in horses, enjoying riding at this recreational level is enough. There's nothing wrong with this, however, don't assume that's all there is to it.

From reading extensively on the subject, I knew there was more to riding, and my desire was to learn as much as I could. But you can't learn it all from books, so I knew I had to find the right coach. I knew I would also have to abandon my comfort zone and move on to other more challenging mounts to improve my skills.

When you move up from a basic pleasure horse to a well-trained dressage schoolmaster, it's like you're suddenly flying a high-tech jet after being seated in a single-engine aircraft for all your past experience. The basic principles remain the same, but the operation requires a whole new, finely honed level of skill to engage the engine and keep it going at optimum performance.

Facing the Fear Factor

Because dressage introduces you to a higher level of horsemanship, the learning experience can dredge up many fears. It's normal to feel afraid of falling off a horse and sustaining injury. Let's face it, horseback riding, like many other sports, is inherently dangerous. Horses have minds of their own and can be unpredictable. They don't always behave the way we expect or want them to. And that ground seems to get harder with each passing year.

Everyone who rides horses feels fearful at some point. For example, it's common to experience fear when getting back on a horse for the first time following a riding accident, especially if the injury required a lengthy recovery. If your level of fitness declined a little during recovery, you may feel even more vulnerable to new injury until your physical stamina returns to normal.

The same is true if you've just been through a long illness that has left you feeling weak and out of shape.

Your horse can sense your vulnerability and may try to take advantage. This happened to me after a yearlong bout with cancer treatment. I continued to ride throughout my ordeal of chemotherapy and radiation, but most days I only felt like putting around the track a few times. My horse enjoyed the light workouts, I'm sure. Problem is, I unwittingly gave her the expectation that this is how nice life could be, and as I grew stronger and began demanding more, she resented having to work harder. As a result, she developed the vice of bolting to escape work, at a time when I was not yet strong and stable enough to maintain effective control. This shook my confidence hard, and although the issue took a long time to resolve, my strength and fitness gradually returned and my skills improved. Ultimately, this incident made me become a better rider, and I was able to restore a positive partnership with my horse.

The life stage at which you start riding makes a difference in how well you handle riding fears, too. Children who start riding at a young age have an advantage here. They seem to gain confidence more quickly because they harbor fewer fears. But for those of us who take up riding as adults, fear can become a major obstacle to our progress. Adults understand better than kids how long it takes to heal from an injury and how much it costs in terms of health care dollars, time lost from work, and so forth. Women burdened with child-care responsibilities are particularly vulnerable to these negative feelings, fearful of leaving their children behind or of being unable to care for them. Adult riders are simply more cognizant of their own mortality and fully aware that a fall from a horse can result in devastating or fatal injury. Fortunately, most riding accidents bruise primarily the rider's ego, but the possibility of serious injury or death is always present.

A certain amount of fear is healthy because it makes you more cautious and safety conscious. But fear also contributes to many riding faults, such as hanging onto the reins, clutching with the legs, not allowing the horse to move forward freely for fear of going too fast, among others.

Horses can sense fear in a rider. In turn, the rider's tension makes the horse tense and uncomfortable, and some may react badly, resorting to spooking, bolting, or any number of other evasive behaviors. Often, the rider doesn't comprehend the true cause and blames the horse. The rider who is too afraid to correct the problem is powerless to overcome it. Part of becoming a thinking rider is learning to recognize when you're letting fear get in the way or hold you back from making progress.

The first step toward recovery is admitting your fear to yourself. Then you will need assistance from an understanding instructor who is willing to work with you and your horse to help restore and build your self-confidence. Be open and honest with your instructor about your fears. There is no shame in having such feelings, except in hiding them. Everyone who has ever ridden extensively has experienced similar feelings at some point in their riding careers, so your issues will be nothing new to your instructor.

If your riding fears are centered around one horse, your instructor may feel it is best for you to ride a different horse for a while, if possible. A return to basics, such as working on your seat on the longe line, may boost your confidence as well. Once you've regained your confidence, brushed up your skills, and learned to relax on the new mount, you need to return to the previous mount to convince yourself that you've conquered your fear. You may be amazed at the difference in the horse's response, now that you're communicating a renewed sense of confidence to him, instead of tension and fear.

Once learned, conquering and controlling fear is a valuable lesson that you will carry with you throughout your riding experience. Fear may revisit you from time to time, as you face new challenges, but having conquered it once, you know you can deal with it. Embrace it and face it as part of the learning process. The effort requires you to push past your comfort zone, which you must do to continue progressing up the levels, where the work gets tougher. When you are ready, your instructor can coach you through the process and challenge you to try new and harder things. But ultimately, it's a matter of resolve on your part to push through the fear, set your goal and reach it. Once you can do this, you are well on your way to becoming a thinking rider who's in control of herself and her horse.

Thinking through Problems

If you want your horse to be correct in his gaits and movements, then your riding must always be correct and thoughtful. A good horse deserves no less. But to do this, you must become skilled enough to school your own mount, keep him tuned up to his current level of training, and resolve any problems that may arise from time to time.

Most problems that horses develop under saddle are because of some fault of the rider. However, when a horse begins to behave badly, the rider often doesn't recognize that his own poor riding habits, lack of skill, or fear may have contributed to the problem, as shown in the figure on the next page. Instead, he blames the horse, the horse's past training, the tack, the windy weather, or whatever.

On the contrary, the thinking rider will always evaluate his own riding and ask, "What am *I* doing to cause this problem?" An educated rider has learned to listen to his horse's body language and other clues that can help him figure out what's wrong, think through the problem, and arrive at the best solution. An educated rider also knows when the solution lies beyond his skill range and when he needs to consult an instructor or trainer to help resolve the problem.

Sometimes, the solution is a simple readjustment of the rider's position or aids that a knowledgeable rider can often fix himself. However, a less skilled rider usually cannot identify the problem properly without help from someone more advanced observing from the ground. In some cases, fixing rider problems may require a refresher course in the basics.

For example, what do you think a horse may be trying to tell his rider when he puts his head down, pulls against the reins, and nearly yanks his rider forward out of the saddle? Probably something like, "Stop grabbing me in the mouth!"

What's wrong with this picture? The rider's hollow back and clenched position has made her horse's back hollow and tense.

Although this problem is nearly always the rider's fault, caused by hanging onto the reins for balance, beginners and nonthinking riders will inevitably blame the horse. Whether the issue arose from lack of skill or loss of confidence, a good instructor recognizes that the rider needs some grounding in the basics. The instructor may decide to put such a rider on the longe line on a trained horse, work on body position, and allow him to concentrate on balancing from a corrected seat, without having to worry about controlling where the horse is going.

The Learning Process

Gradually, as the student gains control over his body position and balance, he works up to riding on the longe line with and without reins, and with and without stirrups at each gait. This helps the student learn to move with and become a unit with the horse in a soft, flexible way. The student also learns to stop the horse with only his seat and weight, which is a great confidence builder. Important for all riders, this fundamental work teaches the student to develop a secure, independent seat without relying on the reins for stability.

Only after the student has learned to feel a correct, independent seat can he discern the difference in balancing off the hands and balancing from a correct body position. Even after learning these lessons well, it is a good idea to drop the irons and ride a little without stirrups during schooling sessions, just to stay in practice. Old habits can easily creep back into play.

Unfortunately, some riding students scoff at longe-line lessons and find them boring or a waste of lesson money. After all, why bother if all you want to do is ride easy trails or hack through the countryside on occasion? The fact is, pleasure riders also need good skills to stay safe and in control when difficult situations arise. Other riders may be scared off by the prospect of riding without reins and stirrups. But these exercises really help the student develop a better seat and gain greater confidence in his riding ability.

For precision riding, hours spent on the longe line honing a secure seat and good balance are a necessary foundation for eventually mastering the more difficult dressage maneuvers. (See the figure on this page for an example of an incorrect seat.) To ride

What's wrong with this picture? This rider's seat is incorrect, as she is leaning slightly back with legs positioned too far forward, as if bracing against the stirrups for support.

well, your body parts—seat, legs, and hands—must function independently, but in a coordinated fashion. You can't rely on your hands and reins for balance when you need them for something else. The independent seat is also much safer, because the more secure you are in the saddle, the more difficult it is for the horse to unseat you, if he is suddenly startled by something, for example, and tries to shy or bolt.

Unfortunately, there are no shortcuts to acquiring these skills. Americans tend to want to rush things—expecting to train a horse or learn to ride in weeks instead of years. Rushing a horse's training can cause him to break down early in his performance career.

Riders also cannot be rushed. Everyone learns at a different pace, so it is impossible to put a time frame around how long it takes to grasp the classical riding principles and graduate to the upper levels. Expect to spend considerable time getting a firm grounding in basic classical skills before attemping fancier maneuvers. Be patient, but if you ever feel like you aren't progressing, enroll in a dressage clinic, try a different instructor, or ride a different school horse for a while to break out of the rut. It's normal, however, to hit plateaus from time to time, kind of like a weight loss program, where you don't see any progress for a while, and then all of a sudden one day you experience a big breakthrough.

Part of becoming a thinking rider is learning to analyze your own and your horse's progress, knowing when to be patient and when to ask for help. Classical training gives you the tools to do so, and it's part of your instructor's job to teach you how to use these tools. You should feel comfortable discussing concerns and questions about your training with your instructor without fear of hurting his feelings. After all, your instructor is a professional who has already traveled the road you're on now and knows what lies ahead. A good instructor delights in a student who works hard, seeks higher knowledge, and demonstrates a passion for the sport.

Beware of the instructor who

- Doesn't teach you to think about what you're doing and why
- Fails to stress the importance of an independent seat or develop it through longe-line work
- Never encourages you to push a little past your comfort zone and try something new
- Never assigns you homework or exercises to practice at home
- Never suggests additional reading

Unfortunately, it's a sad fact that at some barns the training philosophy is to "keep 'em dumb" so that riders will always need the services of a trainer and keep paying for it. This philosophy may make business at the barn more lucrative, but it won't produce many good riders.

Self-Education

Instructors come in all calibers and don't have to be certified to teach riding in the United States. This makes it hard for beginners to know who's naughty and who's nice. It also makes it doubly important for you to seek knowledge on your own and strive to become that thinking rider.

To be a good horseman, and a thinking rider, you must acquire and assimilate a great deal of knowledge on a variety of topics, from horse and pasture care, to veterinary medicine, to saddle fitting, and more. Here are some things you can do to aid your progress:

- Keep a journal of every lesson, show, and horse-related event and review it periodically to reinforce what you're learning.
- Ride as often as you can, daily if possible, or at least every other day.

- Ride as many different horses as possible (they all feel and respond differently, and this gives you a chance to practice "adjusting the volume" of your aids from horse to horse).
- Read books about dressage, especially the ones written by the great riding masters, such as Alois Podhajsky, the former director of the Spanish Riding School in Vienna, Austria (see the "References" section at the back of this book).
- Reread the same dressage books after you've been taking dressage lessons for a while. They will be more meaningful the second time around, after you have a little experience in the subject.
- Learn as much as you can about horsemanship, horse care, horse breeds, rider safety, and related topics through reading or hands-on experience.
- If you don't have the opportunity to care for your own horse at home, volunteer to do barn chores around your boarding stable. You'll learn a lot just by doing the work associated with keeping horses.
- Stay current on dressage competition rules and test requirements, as they change periodically.
- Read the U.S. Equestrian Federation (USEF) *Rule Book* and keep a copy on hand for easy reference (as a USEF member, you can request a printed copy, or you can view the *Rule Book* at www.usef.org).
- Talk to your veterinarian about your horse's nutritional and health care needs.
- Talk to your farrier about your horse's shoeing needs.
- Stay current on equine topics by reading horse magazines.
- Participate in or audit riding clinics, seminars, dressage camps, and similar learning opportunities.

- Observe other instructors and their teaching techniques and try one out from time to time.
- Observe other dressage riders, especially those more advanced than yourself.
- Observe and familiarize yourself with other equestrian sports and disciplines so that you understand the differences and similarities.
- Attend dressage shows and ride-a-tests, either as an exhibitor or as a spectator.
- Volunteer to work in various capacities at a dressage show. Scribing (recording the judge's marks and comments) is an especially good way to learn things from a judge's viewpoint.
- Join a local U.S. Dressage Federation–affiliated dressage chapter or riding club so you can network with others who share your interests.
- Challenge yourself to move out of your comfort zone now and then and attempt something more difficult. Remember, horse and rider both learn best when stressed a little or when slightly challenged to try harder. Certainly, abandoning your comfort zone doesn't mean you should try something that is unsafe or reckless. On the contrary, you should always work with your instructor or an experienced ground person when first attempting any new skill on horseback.

The Thinking Rider as Communicator

The tools we use to communicate with our horses, the aids, have been handed down by horsemen through the centuries and are relatively standard everywhere, with only slight variations. But you can train a horse using any set of cues, voice tones, or hand signals, as long as you apply them consistently. Consistency is crucial to the communication and training process.

Horses have minds of their own, but they aren't mind readers. They don't know what we want them to do unless we teach them what our aids and cues mean. For example, they have no concept of what going straight is. Horses in nature don't walk in straight lines; they meander here and there, looking for the tastier blades of grass. When you get on a green (untrained) horse, he will also try to meander and weave in and out of a straight line, unless you have the skill to make a straight channel with your aids—seat, hands, and legs—and push the horse through it. With aids applied on both sides of the channel, he can't go right or left, so he goes straight. Through repetition, the horse eventually learns that when you get on and apply your aids in this way, he's supposed to go straight forward without wobbling to the left or right. There's a world of difference in riding a green horse like this and riding one that's been well trained to the aids.

To communicate effectively with your horse, you must also understand how he communicates and perceives his world. He may not possess a spoken language like ours, but like all others of his kind, he is a master of body language. To learn this language, observe how horses interact with one another in the field and read books about horse behavior. Applying what you learn will eventually help you win your horse's trust and experience a more enjoyable partnership.

The deep bond and affection that some horse-and-rider pairs share is an intensely joyful and satisfying exchange. Although we can't know for sure what horses feel, it is evident that some dressage horses look forward to their work and seem eager to please their riders. At the core of dressage lies the artistic expression of a truly miraculous harmony between members of two such different species, achieved through a language with no words.

Communicating Leadership

Horses evolved to live in herds for safety in numbers and protection from predators. They possess a strong herd instinct and are most content when kept with other companions, preferably their own kind. As in all social orders, some horses are dominant and assume a leadership role, while others are submissive. It is easy to tell which is which by observing a herd's pecking order in the field at feeding time. The dominant or alpha animal is typically a mare, more often than not, but the ages, physical condition, and personalities of the herd members determine which animal assumes the leadership role.

The other horses will challenge the dominant one from time to time to test her continued worthiness as herd leader. When a new horse is introduced to the herd, everyone has to reestablish roles, and sometimes a new leader may emerge.

In the human-horse relationship, the human must establish himself as the *boss mare*. This is not accomplished through force or fear tactics, but by gaining the horse's trust and being firm and consistent in your handling techniques. Horses feel most secure when following a strong leader who tells them what to do and when something is or isn't safe. This characteristic enabled humans to domesticate the horse. Throughout the ages, we've used this trait to our advantage to train horses to perform all sorts of feats that go against their basic nature, such as jumping through circus hoops of fire.

If you fail to assert yourself as the leader, or if the horse loses his trust in you, he will take charge, and you might not like the results. Horses will also test their human leaders from time to time, just as they will challenge the authority of their herd leader. As a thinking rider, you must be able to recognize when a horse's misbehavior is intended to challenge your authority and be prepared to correct the horse firmly.

For example, if the horse is prancing on his lead rope and trying to drag you around the yard, instead of you leading him, let him know with a swift yank on the lead and a sharp word that his behavior is not acceptable. The same applies under saddle. If the horse is at a halt, but tries to creep forward step by step, you must correct him and make him stand still. An obedient horse should not move until you tell him to with your aids.

Some people are afraid to be firm with their horses, fearing they will ignite worse behavior, such as a bucking spree. Horses, of course, sense this reticence and will challenge your authority or even take charge. After all, who wants to be led by someone who lacks the confidence to lead?

To stay in control, the rider must exude confidence and correct transgressions quickly. Part of your riding instructor's job is to teach you how to make effective corrections, in an acceptable, humane manner, using your aids. Be firm (not cruel) when necessary, but always fair, when doling out corrections. Horses seem to have an innate sense of fairness, and if they feel they are being punished when they don't deserve it, or if they don't understand why they're being punished, they may rebel or lose trust in their handlers.

If you feel fearful in a particular situation, you must control your fear and take care not to communicate your feelings to your horse. Even when you don't feel especially confident, you must possess the self-discipline to exhibit an aura of controlled relaxation around your horse. This is a skill that, in and of itself, takes time to master. Some riders sing or take deep yogalike breaths to calm themselves and refocus. Do whatever works for you to stay calm and in control in a crisis. The reward will be a more obedient horse that respects and trusts you as his leader.

Communicating Trust

Earning your horse's trust requires that you know something about horse psychology, especially his instincts and fears. For example, as an animal of prey, the horse is naturally wary of sudden movements and loud, unfamiliar noises. Such things can easily spook a horse and cause him to shy away from the movement or sound, potentially unseating an inattentive or unskilled rider. At horse shows, you'll often see a horse or two spooked by flash cameras or loud applause. This is why dressage audiences are customarily quiet during a rider's test and why flash photography is sometimes prohibited at shows.

Dogs, too, can be a problem, if the horse is not accustomed to having them around on the farm where he lives. Think about it: In the horse's mind dogs look like wolves, so why wouldn't he instinctively spook and try to run? The horse may be accustomed to living with a dog of a particular color and size, but when confronted with a strange dog of another color or type, he may express fear.

Mother Nature made horses naturally wary of snakes and other dangers lurking in the grass. No wonder that some horses react in fear to ropes and water hoses pulled across the ground. Your horse doesn't know he has no need to be afraid. He's simply reacting out of instinct, until you let him sniff and investigate the object and quietly reassure him that it's okay. If you punish him for acting afraid, you'll only reinforce his fear.

Poles laid out on the ground for training purposes may elicit a similar response. Some horses balk and refuse to go over them the first time. If this happens, lead the horse up to the poles, let him have a good look, reassure him, and then lead him over the poles at the walk, with yourself in front. When he sees you, his leader, going over the poles safely, he likely will follow with no resistance.

Use a similar strategy when getting your horse accustomed to crossing bridges or water obstacles. The horse's survival depends on his feet and legs and his ability to flee from danger. That's why horses are naturally wary of where they put their feet. If they can't see where they're stepping, as in the bottom of a creek bed, they usually won't go there, unless their leader persuades them that it's okay. Similarly, a hollow bridge feels and sounds different from solid ground, so the horse, uncertain of what he's stepping into, will often refuse to cross. When training a horse to trail ride, always take him out the first several times with an older, experienced horse that he can follow across creeks and bridges.

Horses also have a strong homing instinct. This can work in your favor should you ever get lost on the trail or in dense fog. Just give your horse his head, and he'll likely find his way back to his stable. It can also work against you. Horses are so fond of the comforts and security of home that some easily become barn sour. When ridden away from their herd members and familiar territory, the barn sour horse will refuse to continue on, or perhaps even panic, spin around, and try to run back home.

Horses can sense a trap, and this innate survival instinct is why so many are fearful of being loaded into trailers. If a horse willingly follows you into a trailer, then he has learned to trust his human handlers. With this in mind, one should always approach trailer loading and training with utmost care and thoughtfulness. Create positive associations for the horse, such as food rewards for every step up the ramp and a full hay net when he's loaded.

A word of caution here. Keep in mind the obvious and inherent dangers involved in loading a one-ton animal into an enclosure that may make him panic because he suddenly feels trapped. Your own safety around horses is always your primary concern. If you're inexperienced at handling horses or in dealing with specific issues such as trailer loading, seek the help of a more experienced horseman or trainer.

In summary, a large part of the horse's training involves gaining the horse's trust in your leadership. The process of learning how to ride correctly teaches you how to do this, and as your skills and self-confidence improve, so will your horse's trust and confidence in you as a leader. Primarily, the horse has to know that you are not going to hurt him or ask him to do something that he's incapable of doing or that will cause him harm. If he senses fear in you, he may lose trust in what you are asking him to do.

One reason dressage training is broken down into progressively more difficult levels is so that the rider can properly condition and prepare his horse for the next step. If the horse is rushed or forced into attempting a movement before he's ready, he may become frustrated or rebellious. He may also suffer physical trauma if his body isn't properly conditioned for the task. Obviously, this can harm the horse both mentally and physically and damage the rider's relationship with him.

The dressage levels follow a schedule of sorts, so that once a horse (or rider) masters the basics, he's ready to move on to greater challenges. This orderly, time-tested arrangement handed down to us through the centuries by the great equitation masters helps build trust, confidence, and harmony in the magical union of horse and human.

Chapter Five

Choosing a Suitable Dressage Horse

What about Breed?

While warmbloods are favored mounts for upper-level dressage, any horse and any rider can benefit from dressage training. Arabians, Morgans, Thoroughbreds, Quarter Horses, American Saddlebreds, Paints, Norwegian Fjords, and many other breeds have been used as dressage horses. Beatle fans may remember the lovely Appaloosa, Pay N Go, who pranced and performed at the memorial service for Paul McCartney's late wife, Linda. Unlike certain types of horse show classes in which only purebreds can compete, dressage is open to nonpurebred or grade horses, because the horse's ability to perform the required movements of the test is what ultimately counts, not his beauty or bloodline. Such diversity is what makes dressage truly an equal opportunity venture.

In the most simplistic terms, dressage training aims to improve the horse's natural gaits—walk, trot, and canter—and make him a pleasure to ride. To improve in his way of going, the horse is not limited by his breeding, but only by his own natural physical and mental capacity for the discipline. That's why conformation (body structure) and temperament count more than breeding in this sport, and the warmbloods have been bred for centuries to possess the best of these traits that dressage demands.

What exactly is a warmblood? A warmblood is not a specific breed, but a type or category of horse comprised of several different breeds. A *breed* is a group of horses and ponies that are genetically similar and that have been selectively bred to exhibit predictable characteristics.

For example, the Morgan, although not a warmblood, is one of the breeds developed in America bearing common, consistent traits. All Morgans have a common ancestry and can trace their lineage back to one foundation sire called Figure, later renamed Justin Morgan after his owner. Most other breeds developed from more than one foundation sire. The lovely Lipizzaners of Spanish Riding School fame, among the world's most beloved and well-recognized breeds for dressage, trace their roots to six foundation stallions, each with different attributes that remain evident in today's descendants of their bloodlines.

Horse breeds are categorized as being hotbloods, warmbloods, or coldbloods. The hotbloods are the refined riding horse breeds, such as the Arabian, the Thoroughbred, and the American Saddlebred. The coldbloods are the draft horses bred for heavy work, such as the Shire, the Clydesdale, and the Percheron. In simplified terms, the warmblood breeds developed from a cross between the two, resulting in a horse that possesses both strength and refinement. They possess a larger build than most hot-blooded horses, but are not as heavy as the drafts, and are generally considered to be less high strung than the hotbloods.

Some of the better-known warmblood breeds of today include the Holsteiner, the Hanoverian, the Oldenburg, the Westphalian, and the Dutch, Danish, and Swedish Warmbloods. Typically marketed as sport horses, these breeds and other warmbloods are often seen competing in upper-level dressage, where they generally excel because of their natural athleticism and big-moving gaits and because of their tractable dispositions.

Unfortunately, warmblood talent tends to be expensive. This is due partly to the warmblood's suitability for dressage, and partly to its relative rarity in this country, although their numbers have steadily increased as interest in the sport has grown. In fact, more breeders in the United States have begun to selectively develop sport horses of various breeds, not just warmbloods, with dressage horse–type conformation, quality, and movement.

However, not everyone can afford to spend five figures or more for a horse. Plus, some people find the warmblood's big, bounding gaits somewhat difficult and intimidating to ride. Their size and big gaits have a different feel compared to, say, a compactly built Arab or a stocky Quarter Horse. Riding a big-moving warmblood can take some getting used to, because it's a lot of horse to hold together.

The size of the horse is an important consideration and may often be a factor in the price. Most warmbloods are typically large. Some people prefer large horses, while others are more comfortable handling smaller ones. Youngsters may need to start out on a pony. By tradition, a horse is measured in hands from the withers (highest point of the shoulder), with one hand equaling four inches. A pony is a full-grown equine that stands 14 hands 2 inches and under.

Purebreds tend to be more expensive than grade horses, or nonpurebreds. However, a warmblood pedigree alone, or any other pedigree, for that matter, doesn't guarantee success in the show ring. Therefore, cost and riding ability aside, the type of horse you buy really depends on what your dressage goals are and on how serious a rider you become as you get more involved in the sport. As you progress in your skills, you may find it necessary to change horses from time to time. If you're determined to reach the upper levels in dressage and learn the more complicated maneuvers, then invest in the best horse, preferably a dressage schoolmaster, and the best instructor that you can find and afford.

If you simply want to dabble in dressage for a while to see whether you like it or to improve your flat work for another equestrian discipline, then stick with the horse you already have. Or shop for the type of mount that you feel most comfortable and confident riding. The two of you may remain in the lower levels, but you'll both improve and work better together for the effort. Plus, the added confidence that dressage training instills in both horse and rider will make your overall riding much more pleasurable.

Why It's Best to Learn from a Schoolmaster

If you're serious about dressage and are intent on competing at the higher levels someday, you should, if at all possible, dig deep into your pockets and purchase or lease a quiet schoolmaster to learn on. A schoolmaster is a made or finished horse that has been correctly schooled in the classical principles. Generally an older, retired show horse, the ideal schoolmaster is one who possesses a patient, suitable temperament for tolerating unskilled riders who have not yet mastered the art of good hands and good seat. Tolerance is a necessity, as not all horses are cut out to be teachers. In fact, some highly trained horses are easily vexed by a novice rider's repeated mistakes and will not tolerate flapping legs, bouncing butts, rough hands, or other perceived abuses. They can figure out very quickly when they have a beginner on their back and often will take advantage.

If you can't find or afford a schoolmaster, then take lessons as often as possible on someone else's schoolmaster. Don't start out with a young horse and expect to train it. Green horses and green riders are never a good mix. Even if you've worked in another equestrian discipline for years and know how to ride, and your horse is well trained in that discipline, you're both still considered beginners in dressage. You will learn and progress faster on a trained dressage horse that already knows what to do, instead of trying to train your horse as you learn.

For a beginner, acquiring a horse that is around 10 to 14 years old is ideal. At this age, the horse has likely already been trained up and accustomed to different situations, such as horse shows and riding trails. Many dressage horses that are well cared for can still perform into their 20s, barring accidents and disease. A novice rider should not even consider acquiring a young horse under age 5. Horses mature at around age 4 and usually aren't even ridden until around age 2 or 3, so a 5-year-old just hasn't been around long enough to have had a lot of under-saddle training invested in him.

As you might guess, schoolmasters aren't cheap. This is because someone else has already spent countless hours developing the horse's talent and probably also campaigning him on the show circuit. But as you write the check, consider that you're investing in your dressage education by buying a four-legged professor who can share a lifetime of training and knowledge with you. A good schoolmaster, like a good instructor, knows more than you do about the sport in the beginning and can help you realize your dressage dreams in time.

Your schoolmaster should be working several levels above where you are starting your riding instruction. For example, if you're starting at Introductory or Training Level dressage, you want to learn on a schoolmaster that's at least a solid Third or Fourth Level horse, or higher. The horse also must be lesson sound—able to be ridden regularly without pain or discomfort. Although he likely will be past the age at which he can compete rigorously on a full season show circuit, you'll want him to be sound enough to take to a few local schooling or recognized shows to test your progress.

One final warning: Many people harbor the misconception that a schoolmaster is a push-button horse and that once they acquire a well-trained horse, they can just jump on and start half-passing and pirouetting all over the place. I'm here to tell you that it doesn't work that way at all, and no such push-button creature exists in the equine world. Even high-level horses don't dance unless you, as a well-educated rider, know how to push the right buttons. If you've never done dressage before, you must still spend considerable time in the saddle learning how to coordinate and apply the aids precisely and properly for each movement. Remember, dressage is all about precision riding. Nothing in

The Benefits of Leasing a Horse

If you've never owned a horse before, leasing one is a good way to discover whether you truly will enjoy the commitment of horse ownership. Often, people are surprised and dismayed to learn how much time and work is involved in owning a horse. After a few months, some people lose interest in their new horse or find they don't have time for the work associated with riding, and the horse begins to suffer from lack of attention. Leasing gives you an opportunity to experience the commitment of keeping a horse on a short-term basis, so you can better decide whether you want to make it a long-term commitment.

Horses to lease generally aren't advertised. To find out about them, you have to ask your instructor or other horse people in your community to be on the lookout and let you know if they hear of someone willing to lease their horse for a period of time. Check with local riding establishments, as some barns will lease their school horses off season to keep them ridden and in shape. Some establishments even arrange

dressage is as push-button simple or as easy as it looks. But a schoolmaster can make your learning process decidedly easier, because he'll understand what you want (having already been taught the movement), once you figure out how to ask him for it correctly. Whereas an untrained horse won't have a clue what you're talking about, even if you do apply the aids correctly.

At the outset, a dressage schoolmaster is supposed to know more than his rider, and you'll know from his responses whether you're riding correctly. So prepare to be humbled at times, even if you've been riding for a while. It will take time to develop the feel, balance, and sensitivity necessary to command a good dressage performance on a well-educated horse.

time-share agreements with riders who take lessons on their school horses.

Have your riding instructor evaluate any leasing prospect that interests you to help ensure that the mount is safe, suited to your abilities, and sound enough for your purposes. If the horse is for sale, leasing him for a short time will give you an opportunity to get to know him better, discover any little quirks, and decide whether he's the horse for you. Many a good match has been made this way.

The leasing agreement should spell out your responsibilities as well as the horse owner's. For example, who will pay the board, vet, and farrier bills? What type of insurance is required, and who is responsible for any liability issues, such as personal injury or property damage, that may occur during the term of the lease? Aside from length of lease and payment terms, the agreement should also clearly state whether anyone else, including the owner, can ride the horse, and whether the horse can be transported to trails, shows, or other events.

Searching for a Horse

Novice riders are wise to take lessons for at least six months or longer before they consider leasing or buying their first horse. For safety, you need to know how to handle horses and be comfortable around them before you acquire one of your own. When you feel ready, and the time comes to look for a horse of your own, your riding instructor is the best place to start. Your instructor knows your riding ability and can help you try out and select a horse that will be a good match.

Another alternative is to solicit the help of a horse professional as a broker or consultant to locate and evaluate horses for you to try. High-dollar horses are typically bought and sold in this way through an agent. If not your instructor, then the person who helps you hunt for a horse must be someone you know and trust or who has been recommended to you by someone you trust. You can expect to pay either a flat fee or a percentage for this person's time and expertise, but your chances of selecting a safe, sound, and suitable mount will be greatly improved.

The Internet, newspapers, and trade journals advertise horses for sale all the time, but these are not the best places to start, unless you are already a competent horse person in your own right and experienced in the buying and selling of horses. Unfortunately, there are many dishonest people in the horse-trading business who will stoop to doping horses to conceal lameness or use other unsavory tactics to hide physical or behavioral problems.

Knowing What to Look for in a Dressage Horse

As is true when selecting any companion animal, buying a horse should never be an impulse decision. Nor should you let issues such as color and markings be deciding factors. Paints and Palominos are pretty horses, but choose a horse for what he's been trained to do and for what you can learn from him, not for how he appeals to the eye or to your tastes in color. The more horses you try out the better. Individual horses move and feel differently under saddle. By riding a variety of horses, you may find that you prefer a lean, narrow animal to a wide-barreled one; or the gaits of a smaller, shorter horse may be easier for you to ride than those of a big-strided, massively tall mount.

Some people prefer geldings (castrated male horses) over mares (females). Mares sometimes experience mood swings and behavioral changes during their estrus cycles that can make them more unpredictable when they're in season. Either sex is suitable for dressage, however, only the most accomplished horseman should ride and handle stallions (intact males).

Expect to invest considerable time in your search for a suitable dressage mount. Some travel and overnight stays may also be involved when trying out horses. If your consultant goes with you on these trips, you will be expected to pay his expenses. Think of your search as hiring an equine instructor and make the interview process as detailed and lengthy as you need it to be. When you take time to shop around, you're more likely to select a mount that will be a good match for your riding goals and abilities. The horse you select can make or break your prospects of becoming an accomplished dressage rider. Getting the wrong horse, unsuited to your abilities, can cause you to lose your confidence or otherwise disappoint and discourage further interest in the sport.

Whenever possible, weed through the prospects by viewing videos. Then arrange to visit and ride only the ones that really interest you. On the day of your test ride, ask the current owner (or the person showing you the horse) to ride him first. Watch how the horse behaves and moves under saddle. Then ask your instructor or consultant to ride and evaluate him before you try him out yourself.

You may wish to ride the horse more than once before you make up your mind, preferably at different times of the day. Like people, some horses work better in the morning than later in the day, or vice versa. Be sure to observe the horse's behavior during routine handling and tacking up. You will pick up many clues about the horse's overall disposition and willingness to please simply by watching him have his hooves picked out and be groomed, saddled, and bridled.

Above all, when you find a horse you like, don't buy him on the spot. Take time to evaluate him. Ask why he's being sold, ascertain as much as you can about his background, have him vet checked, and compare him to other horses. A legitimate seller will not try to pressure you into buying a horse on the spot, so don't fall for ploys intended to get you to make a hasty decision.

Assessing Gaits and Movement

To be a suitable dressage mount, a horse must have pure gaits at the walk, trot, and canter. That is, you must hear four distinct beats at the walk, two distinct beats at the trot, and three distinct beats at the canter. If, for example, you can hear four beats at the canter, then that horse's gait is incorrect. The walk and trot should show no signs of pacing, which occurs when both legs on the same side of the body move forward simultaneously. Certain faults in a gait can be corrected with training, but you'll need a knowledgeable and experienced trainer's assessment to determine whether it's worth the effort and risk.

Tracking Up

Another way to assess a horse's gait is to observe how well he tracks up, or steps into or over the tracks of his front feet. Tracking up is easiest to see at the walk. Circle the horse on a longe line and watch the spot on the ground where the inside foreleg leaves a hoofprint. The horse's inside hind leg should over stride this spot by five or six inches or more at the walk. At the trot, a relaxed horse that is moving forward freely should track right into the hoofprints left by his front feet.

Straightness

The horse should also track straight—that is, the hind feet should follow in line with the front feet, even on the arc of a circle. As you can see in the figure on the next page, although bent on the circle's arc, the horse on the right is traveling straight on the circle, because his hind feet follow in line with his forefeet. The horse on the left is crooked on the circle, with hindquarters falling in, and with no bend on the arc, making it impossible for the hind feet to follow in the footsteps of the forefeet. This is easiest to see by observing the horse move both toward you and away from you on a straight line. Moving straight toward you, you should not see the horse's hind feet falling out to either side of the front. Likewise, when watching him from

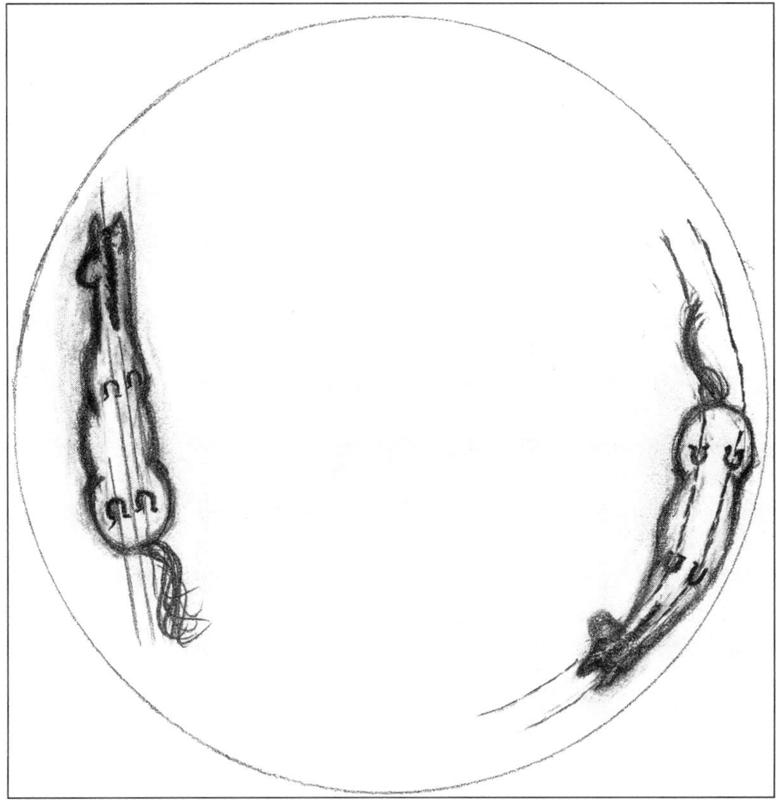

The horse on the right is traveling straight on the arc of the circle, with hind feet following the front, while the horse on the left is actually going crooked.

behind, you should not see the front feet landing to either side of the hind.

Nearly all horses have some degree of natural crookedness, and it is up to the rider to maintain straightness by sitting and riding correctly, and applying effective aids to keep the horse moving straight (see the figure on the next page). Just as people are either right-handed or left-handed, horses, too, have a favored side, and it is usually easier for them to go straighter on their best side. That's why during schooling sessions the rider should work the horse in both directions to ensure that the muscles on both sides of the horse's body develop evenly.

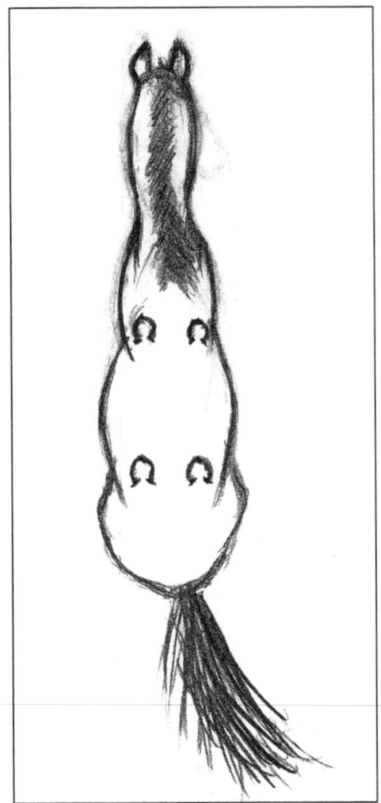

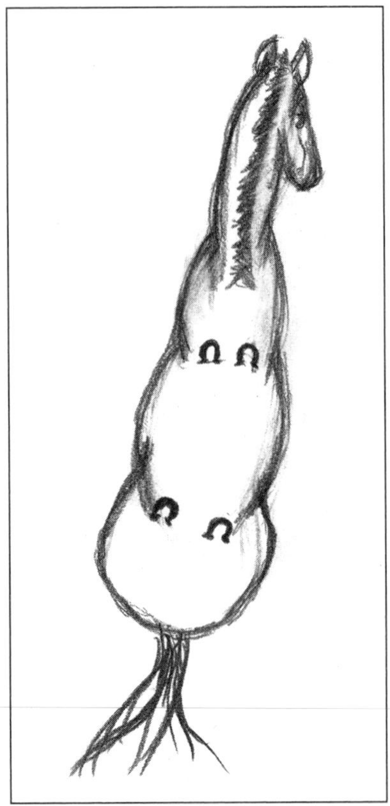

A horse is moving straight (left) when his hind feet follow in line with his front feet, even on a circle. Most horses are crooked (right) to a degree and must be ridden correctly to go straight.

The Prepurchase Exam

Never invest in a dressage prospect without first having him vetted to ensure that he's healthy and sound enough for the job you want him to do (see the figure on page 124, which shows the points of the horse). The prospective buyer pays the cost of the prepurchase exam. This is money well spent to help ensure that your purchase comes with no unpleasant surprises.

If possible, be present when the veterinarian examines the horse. Explain to the vet exactly how you intend to use the horse, including whether you plan to show, event, trail ride, jump, breed the horse, and so forth. If the horse has an expensive price tag, it's a good idea to have all four legs and feet X-rayed. Because of the hindquarter engagement demanded in dressage, older performance horses often have some degree of arthritic changes in their hocks. So it's smart to X-ray these two joints at least, if you don't want to spend the money for a full set of pictures. These days, most X-rays can be done in the barn.

Don't expect to find a perfect horse, because none exists. The veterinarian will list any faults she finds. These faults may or may not affect the way you plan to ride and use the horse. It is up to you and your instructor to evaluate the vet's findings, determine whether a particular fault may negatively impact your riding goals, and decide what shortcomings you can accept and cope with reasonably.

For example, an aged schoolmaster may not score perfectly on the flexion test, a simple procedure used to evaluate leg joint soundness. As mentioned, most older horses have some arthritic changes or other age-related issues. However, there are degrees of lameness, and while a less than satisfactory score may render the horse unsuitable for rigorous show circuit campaigning or other hard competitive work, such as eventing, he may be serviceably sound enough for riding lessons on the flat and general pleasure riding. Don't discount him entirely if you're looking for something to learn on, with the intention of moving up to a younger, more competitive horse later, as your riding skills improve.

My own schoolmaster was missing an eye when I bought her, the result of an injury that happened when she was young. Technically, this is an unsoundness, and I'm sure some people thought I was crazy for buying a half-blind horse. But from a practical standpoint, horses having loss of sight in either eye may still compete in dressage. This particular mare was very quiet, well mannered, a good mover, and well trained in the classical principles. She had been shown successfully in the past. Plus, she was no more easily startled on the blind side than on the sighted side, nor was she quirky about being handled or approached on the blind side.

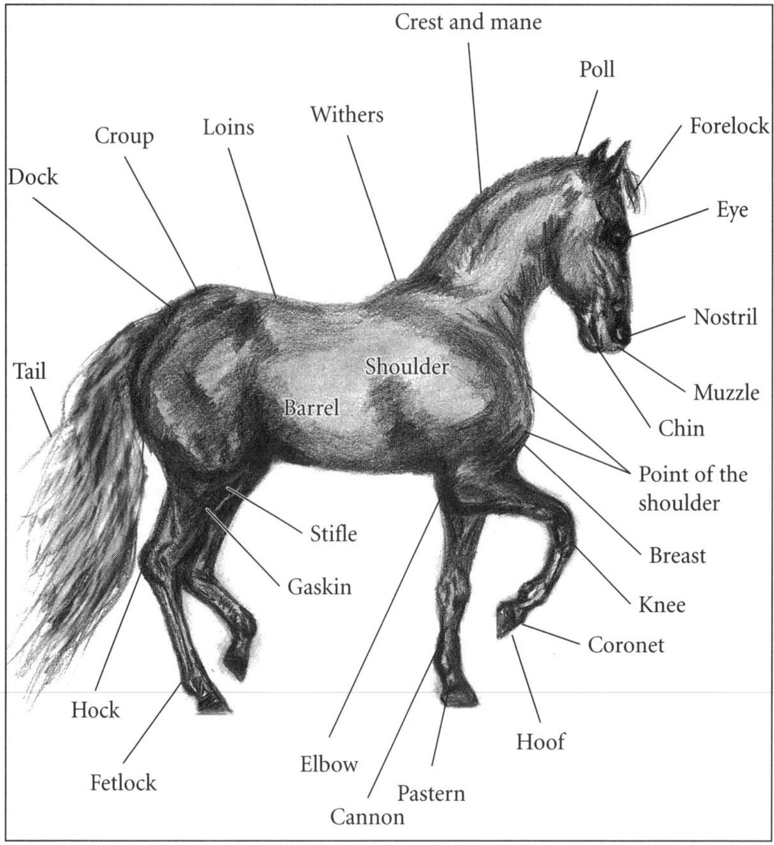

The points of the horse.

My instructor and I weighed the pros and cons carefully and decided that the missing eye was something we could live with. The mare's temperament and training made her a valuable lesson horse, suitable for my purposes, and the missing eye made her talent reasonably priced and suitable for my pocketbook. So I purchased her for what she could do, and for what I could learn from her, not for how she looked. Ultimately, the choice was a good one, because she taught me a great deal and helped me develop the confidence to ride big-moving warmblood types.

EVALUATING CONFORMATION

The one time you should be concerned about how a horse looks is when you're evaluating conformation. But again, conformation does not mean how pretty the horse is, but how well his bones and muscles are conformed structurally to do the job you want him to do. A horse with good conformation will be pleasing to the eye because he is built well proportioned. Also, a horse that is put together well will be a better mover, have better balance overall, and possess greater endurance.

Too vast a topic to cover here, conformation is a complex subject about which volumes have been written. Therefore, you are wise to have a horse professional evaluate the body build of any animal that you are interested in purchasing. Your instructor can evaluate how well the horse is built to do dressage. A veterinarian can evaluate potential soundness issues related to the horse's conformation. For example, a horse with short, upright pasterns and feet that are too small in proportion to the rest of his body is more likely to develop navicular disease later in life.

Obviously, the forelegs should be straight with feet pointing forward, not toeing out or in. Evaluate the hocks carefully, as they must flex well and bear the horse's weight on the hind end in dressage. It is not uncommon for older dressage horses to exhibit varying degrees of hock problems because of the demands that have been placed on them through the years. The hind legs should stand under the horse in a balanced manner, but not too far under and not camped out behind him. When looking at the horse from behind, there should be no deviation through the hock either inward or outward to the hoof.

The ideal dressage horse is built slightly uphill. That is, the withers are slightly higher than the croup, and the neck is attached and carried high. It is much easier for an uphill-built horse to get his haunches under himself. Not so for the downhill horse, who is croup-high and whose neck is attached and carried low. Many Quarter Horses and Thoroughbreds have downhill conformation because this build fosters greater speed. This is not a conformation fault, but simply a difference in the way the horse is conformed to do the job he was originally bred to do.

Certainly, this doesn't mean that Quarter Horses and Thoroughbreds aren't suitable for dressage. Many compete quite well and are popular mounts for the sport, especially at the lower levels, where they typically outnumber the warmbloods because they are less expensive to acquire.

Good conformation is important, but it isn't everything. Remember, there is no perfect horse. And often, minor faults can be corrected or compensated for through proper training and riding, or sometimes even through proper tack or corrective shoeing, depending on the defect.

Evaluating Temperament

Temperament *is* everything in dressage. You want a horse that behaves well and is easy to handle at home, at shows, or in other unfamiliar places. Dressage can be as mentally demanding to the horse as it is to the rider. The dressage horse must possess a good mind and a willing disposition to be able to accept the demands of precision training. His temperament must be tractable and trusting enough for him to attempt anything his rider asks of him. Of course, the rider must always reward that trust by never asking more of the horse than he is capable of doing at each stage of development.

On occasion, all horses will spook or behave badly when frightened. This is natural for an animal of prey whose first line of self-defense is to flee the scene. You want a horse that trusts his rider enough to listen, obey, and settle promptly when spoken to in a calm, soothing manner. Definitely avoid horses that are known to possess confirmed vices, such as rearing, bucking, kicking, or biting, as these animals are dangerous and require expert handling and retraining.

All horses may bite or kick at each other from time to time, when competing for food, for example, or even when romping and socializing with one another. Some horses will kick when followed too closely by another horse, although this is more the rider's fault for not pacing his mount at least one horse length behind the one in front.

An otherwise calm and mild-mannered mare may undergo profound temperament changes while she's in estrous and behave in unexpected ways. Estrous occurs approximately every twenty-eight days and is most evident in early spring. A stallion around a mare in heat has only one thing on his mind and may become unruly, which is why intact males should be handled only by experienced horsemen.

When directed at human handlers, however, these natural behaviors can become a dangerous vice. A well-placed kick from a horse can break bones or even kill. A bite from a horse's powerful jaws can amputate fingers or cause other serious injury. Horses generally give warning before they strike by pinning their ears flat against their heads, so be aware of such signs, especially when working around horses you do not know well.

Cribbing and wood chewing are other vices you want to avoid. *Cribbing* is the habit of gripping a vertical object, such as a fence rail, and gulping air. The vice can lead to health and dental problems and is extremely difficult to break once well established. Teeth marks and gnawed areas on fencing and stall rails indicate a cribber or wood chewer. Although these vices aren't dangerous to humans, they are annoying and unhealthy for the horse, as well as your pocketbook, as you can be held responsible for the damage your horse causes at a boarding stable.

Chapter Six

Caring for Your Dressage Horse

What You Need to Know

The discipline of dressage goes far beyond the arena. It involves managing your horse's health, both physical and mental, to help ensure that the horse maintains optimum fitness and soundness. To do so, the horse owner must:

- Understand good stable and pasture management
- Read and learn about equine health and diseases
- Keep up with the latest research on equine health
- Keep accurate equine health records
- Maintain a regular vaccination and parasite control program
- Learn to identify problems
- Be prepared to handle emergencies
- Know when to call the vet

Boarding Your Dressage Horse

Primary stabling requirements for horses include adequate shelter from the elements, ample pasture, and strong, safe fencing.

Although the climate of your region will dictate the type of shelter your horse will need, generally speaking your choices range from fancy as a fine stable with indoor plumbing and electricity to simple as a sturdy, three-sided shed.

Whatever the arrangement, a dressage performance horse, or any horse, for that matter, should not be left standing in a stall all day without exercise or turnout into a pasture or paddock. Some people keep their horses stabled around the clock for security or protection or because they have no other option. However, the boredom that ensues from such an imprisoning lifestyle can foster detrimental vices and behavioral problems, such as cribbing (wind-sucking), wood chewing, stall weaving, and bursts of pent-up energy on release.

For older horses in particular, the constant standing in a confined space, coupled with the lack of exercise, can aggravate stiff joints and cause "stocking up," a condition where fluid pools in the limbs (usually the hind) and causes swelling. If little or no turnout is available, and circumstances dictate that the horse remain in a stall, the horse owner must make arrangements for the animal to be ridden, hand-walked, or exercised daily.

Your horse will be happier and healthier if you can keep him in as near natural conditions as possible. This means giving him regular and ample turnout time on grass and the opportunity to romp and socialize freely with other herd members (as shown in the figure on the next page). Horses evolved to be grazing herd animals, constantly walking and moving about as they nibble grass throughout the day. Nature never intended for them to be cooped up and fed two concentrated meals a day. However, the way we use horses for showing and other purposes often dictates that they be kept this way, more for the convenience of the owner than for the health and welfare of the horse.

My own horses stay out twenty-four hours a day when weather conditions permit. They have access to a simple run-in shed for shelter from wind and rain. As the seasons change, however, they may occupy their box stalls at night during the coldest part of winter or during the hottest and buggiest part of summer. But

Horses are happiest when allowed turnout time with compatible herd companions. This mare and foal seem content in their paddock.

they spend most of their lives outdoors contentedly grazing with their pasture companions. My aged dressage schoolmaster seems happiest and fittest living this way. In fact, she becomes stiff, stressed, and anxious after being confined to a stall for too long a time.

Horses spend their lives in our service and, therefore, deserve to be comfortable, well cared for, and protected. But as much as your particular situation allows, they should also be permitted to enjoy life as a horse and not be forced to stay confined all day in a twelve-by-twelve-foot box stall without exercise. Be sure to consider these issues carefully when deciding about stabling arrangements for your own horse.

Benefits of Boarding

Owning property on which to house a horse may make horsekeeping somewhat less expensive and more convenient in terms of having your horse close by to see everyday. However, there are some definite benefits to boarding at a reliable, well-run facility, especially for the first-time horse owner:

- Someone else does the work—cleans stalls, buys feed, maintains grounds and fencing, and feeds and waters the livestock. This is primarily what you pay for.
- Someone else is there to tend to your horse when you're out of town or on vacation.
- Your horse will be in the company of other horses. This is important because horses are highly social herd animals, and they need the companionship of their own kind.
- You will have an opportunity to meet and observe other horse people and learn from them. This can be especially beneficial if you're fortunate enough to find a facility that caters exclusively to dressage riders.
- You probably will have a knowledgeable stable manager or other experienced horseman on hand to consult when you encounter problems.

Some disadvantages of boarding that you must consider in your decision include the expense, the drive time to and from the stable, and the real possibility that, at some time in the future, you may be asked to leave and find somewhere else to keep your horse. The latter could happen for any number of reasons, for example, if the facility is sold or goes out of business. The agreement you sign with any boarding facility should spell out the terms of prior notice to be given on the part of either party, whether you are forced to vacate the premises or you simply opt to leave voluntarily.

Selecting a Boarding Facility

If you don't own land where you can keep a horse, scout out a suitable boarding facility *before* you buy a horse. That way, you can arrange for your horse to have a new home ready and waiting for him, as soon as you hand over the check to the seller. You can choose from a commercial boarding facility, where horsekeeping, riding instruction, and related activities are the owner's primary business. Or you may select a private farm, where the owner is willing to rent you a stall and pasture to offset the cost of keeping his own livestock. A private facility is not always the best choice for a beginning rider or first-time owner, unless some quality instruction and a riding arena where you can safely practice your skills are available for your use on or near the premises.

Regardless of whether it's a private or commercial barn, the boarding facility where you choose to house your horse should be clean and well maintained. Select a boarding facility where the owner, stable manager, or attendant lives or works full time on the premises. Horses need to be checked on at least twice a day and fed and watered regularly. If your horse is rugged, someone should check his blanket periodically to make sure it hasn't slipped loose or that it isn't rubbing sore spots on his body. These kinds of services are what you're paying for when you can't be there to do it yourself.

You're also paying for the routine chores and physical labor associated with tending a farm and livestock. For example, your horse's stall must be cleaned daily, and the bedding replenished regularly. Water buckets must be dumped, cleaned, and refilled. In winter, water buckets and outdoor troughs must be kept ice free so that horses have ready access to fresh water at all times. Horse pastures need to be mowed and maintained. Obviously, the caretaker must be a responsible and knowledgeable horse person. To make sure, ask about the caretaker's credentials. How long has he been involved with horses and with what riding disciplines? Preferably, you want someone looking after your horse who understands the needs of dressage and performance horses. Talk to other boarders and find out how satisfied they are with the facility and how long they've been boarding there. Also, find out what you can about the history of the facility, how long it has been in operation, how long under the same ownership, how long under prior owners, and so forth.

Pasture Board

Depending on your finances, you may choose pasture board only, which is less expensive than full board. Full board usually means that your horse gets a stall with pasture turnout, but arrangements may vary in different parts of the country, depending on the climatic conditions.

Pastures at the facility you select should be well maintained and rotated occasionally to permit parasites to die off and to allow the grass to recover, if overgrazing occurs. Fields where horses are kept should also be free of holes, debris, machinery, poisonous plants (ask your local agricultural extension agent for a list), and other hazards. Fencing should be sturdy, well maintained, and suitable for horses. Clean and abundant water must be readily available, preferably via a large watering trough.

The field where your horse will stay should have free access to shelter for shade and protection from wind and the elements. The field and the shelter need to be big enough to accommodate the number of animals kept there, as overcrowding may result in injuries from kicking. Generally speaking, at least two acres of pasture per animal is preferable.

The Riding Arena

Another area you need to carefully evaluate when selecting a stable is the arena where you will ride and school your horse. For safe and proper schooling, the size and footing of the arena are particularly important for the dressage horse. A standard dressage arena is 20 by 60 meters (66 by 198 feet), and a small arena is 20 by 40 meters (66 by 131 feet), so your practice area should be at least this size or larger. This will give you plenty of room to practice your dressage patterns and figures. Barns catering to dressage riders usually post the letters around the arena at the designated sites so you can easily spot your patterns and practice actual tests.

Looking at an Arena's Features

If the outdoor arena is lighted, you will be able to ride after sunset. This is an important consideration for folks who work full-time day jobs and can only ride in the evenings after work and on weekends.

Some larger facilities have indoor and outdoor arenas. This is certainly a plus, as an indoor arena allows you to ride and school year round, regardless of weather conditions or hours of daylight. But you can expect to pay a higher boarding fee to defray the additional maintenance costs of an indoor riding ring.

If a barn houses primarily hunters and jumpers, find out whether riders are required to remove their jumps after each use. If jumps remain set up in the arena most of the time, your use of the ring will be limited for dressage. That's one good reason finding a barn where the needs of dressage riders predominate will ultimately prove more beneficial and convenient for you. Another good reason is the unique camaraderie you will share with other dressage riders who understand the joys and frustrations inherent in this difficult sport. Also, watching the more advanced riders school their horses will enrich your educational experience in dressage. They may even be willing to act as your mentors.

Although rare in regions where land use grows more restricted every year, access to trails or open fields where you may obtain permission to ride is a real privilege, if available. Hacking out on occasion is a refreshing experience for most horses, as well as a good way for you to build confidence and enjoy your riding skills. However, if you're new to riding, or your horse has never been ridden on trails or in open, unfamiliar territory, you should not venture away from the barn alone.

Many horses become anxious and harder to handle when removed from familiar surroundings and the security of their herd. Ones that have grown especially barn sour may panic and attempt to run back to the barn. The rider must be skilled enough to deal with this behavior.

Because riding alone is never wise, invite along one of your more experienced barn buddies who has a quiet, proven trail horse that can help yours relax and settle into the new experience. Trails pose a number of potential hazards, so carry a cell phone with you in case of emergencies.

Evaluating a Riding Arena's Footing

Because horses did not evolve to carry a hundred pounds or more on their backs while performing pirouettes and tempi changes, the type of arena surface on which you spend many hours schooling is critical for your horse's long-term soundness. The dressage horse needs a level, well-drained, well-cushioned surface with good traction.

An arena surface that is too hard provides little or no shock absorption for the hooves as they strike the ground. Eventually, too-hard footing can cause concussion injuries to the feet, legs, and joints, resulting in lameness. A surface that is too soft or deep is not good either, because the extra effort required to wade through it adds stress and strain on tendons and ligaments.

Although grass looks nice, it is slippery when too wet or too dry. A grass arena is also difficult to keep level. In soft, damp earth, horses' feet sink in and create dips in the ground called divots. When the ground dries, these shallow holes or bumpy depressions remain and can cause injury due to strains, sprains, and stumbling.

The arena base is typically clay, stone dust, or fine gravel. The base acts as a protective layer, keeping rocks, roots, and other debris from working their way into the surface footing that tops it. The layer over the base can be a mixture of materials, such as sand, top soil, sawdust, wood chips, and rubber (made from recycled tires) or fiber additives. Whatever material is used, the surface layer must be laid down several inches deep so that it provides suitable cushioning and traction for the horse's feet.

Dust is the most common complaint about riding arena footings, especially in indoor arenas and in hot, dry weather conditions. Regular watering with a hose or sprinkler system is the most common remedy, but there are also dust-control additives that can be applied.

Because of the dust factor, indoor arenas must have good ventilation. Even after wetting the surface layer, good ventilation is necessary to dissipate the fine particles of sand and soil churned up by the horse's hooves. Otherwise, horse and rider may breathe in too much arena dust and develop respiratory problems.

Safety First

When evaluating any private or commercial boarding facility, safety should be high on your list of critical criteria. A well-run stable sells itself, because it appears neat and well organized. Aisles are swept and kept clear of trash and equipment. Tack and grooming supplies are stored out of the way in the tack room or in trunks or closets. Sharp implements, such as rakes and pitchforks, are stored out of the way when not in use. Children are not permitted to run and roughhouse around the horses or near the riding arena. Dogs stay on a leash or under their owners' control. No Smoking signs are posted in and around the barn and are strictly enforced. A fire extinguisher or a hose and faucet are easily accessible inside the barn.

Practical Considerations

Other things you need to consider when selecting a stabling facility include how far you are willing to drive to care for and ride your horse. If you aren't able to drive to the barn daily, you will need to visit several times a week to ensure your horse's wellbeing. Remember, the boarding facility feeds horses and cleans out stalls, but grooming and exercise are typically the owner's responsibility unless you make other arrangements. On occasion, you may also need to meet your veterinarian or farrier there to see your horse. Horse ownership is a full-time commitment, so don't count on showing up at the barn only when you feel like riding.

The private barn where I board my own horses is a thirty-five-minute drive from my home. That distance is minor to me, however, because the stable is well managed by a knowledgeable and trustworthy person, the horses are well cared for, the riding arena has excellent footing, and the pastures are spacious and well maintained. Best of all, my riding instructor comes there to teach, because most of the boarders are her dressage students. There are other stables closer to my home, but all these factors combined make the extra distance worthwhile to me. Besides, I've learned to use the drive time to mentally rehearse the arena exercises I intend to practice that day.

When making your decision about where to keep a horse, be sure to consider whether the barn's hours of operation will coincide with your schedule. Will you be able to visit and ride your horse any time you like or only during certain hours? Some facilities are more restrictive than others about when boarders can come and go.

If your riding instructor can coach at the facility, that's a big plus. You can receive lessons on your own horse without having to trailer him elsewhere. Not all barns permit outside trainers to teach at their facility, so this is something you need to ascertain beforehand.

Secure and Safe Containment

Regardless of where you decide to keep your horse, the facility must be able to safely and securely contain him within sturdy, well-constructed buildings and fences. Run-down fencing and ramshackle sheds pose the hazards of injury and invite horses to escape. A horse running loose is a disaster waiting to happen, especially if near a busy highway. Be aware that as a horse owner, you are liable for any injuries and property damages your horse may cause if, for example, he gets out on the road and is hit by a car.

Fencing

Whether you stable your horse on your own property or at a boarding facility, the fencing should be high (at least four feet), easily visible (horses need to be able to see their boundary lines), sturdy, and safe enough for horses. Depending on where you live, wooden or plastic rail, electric braided wire, metal pipe fencing, or diamond mesh wire with a rail across the top (so the horses can see it) may be more common in your area. But you definitely

Wooden fencing requires painting and upkeep but is considered safe and suitable for containing horses when it is well maintained.

should not subject your horse to barbed wire fencing, as horses can suffer serious injuries if they get tangled in a loose, snarling strand. Also avoid high tensile (strong) wire; if the horse gets caught in it and puts up a struggle, it can saw through tendons, ligaments, and even bone without breaking. While strong fencing is desirable for containing livestock, you still want a type that will break if the horse happens to run through it or become entangled. This is why wooden fencing, shown in the figure on this page, is often the material of choice.

Stalls

A box stall should be big enough, at least twelve by twelve feet or larger, for the average-sized horse to turn around and lie down in comfortably without getting cast (stuck with feet against the wall and unable to rise). The stall should be dry, well bedded, and well ventilated with fresh air, but not with direct drafts blowing on the horse.

If the stall is built of wood, the boards must be close enough together to ensure that your horse cannot stick his head or hoof through a gap and get stuck. Inspect the stall's interior regularly to make sure there are no nails working out or other sharp protruding objects on which your horse could scrape or cut himself.

Even when confined to a stall, horses need to be able to see other horses to satisfy their social and herd instincts. The stall should have a window for the horse to see out; however, to prevent injuries a screen or metal grid must separate the horse from the glass pane. Ideally, the stall should be fully enclosed with closely spaced bars or metal gridwork starting halfway up and extending to the ceiling. This way, the horse can see what's going on around him or socialize with his buddy in the stall next door. But he cannot stick his nose through the bars or gridwork to pick on his neighbor or swing his head over the stall door to nip at visitors and create mischief.

Manure Management

If you keep your horse at home, you'll have to clean up after him daily, as horses produce a lot of waste. If you board, this is one of those chores that you pay some other willing person to do. But effective manure management is important because it aids in the control and spread of parasites, both in the barn and in the pasture. Your horse's health will suffer if the premises are not kept clean.

The tools of the trade include a shovel or manure fork and a wheelbarrow. Scoop out all droppings and urine-soaked bedding in the stall, and replace with fresh, dry bedding as needed.

Most stables establish a manure pile where waste is composted and periodically hauled to the dump or spread on the fields as fertilizer. The compost pile should be located outdoors in a sunny area. Sunlight helps to dry and age the material and destroy parasites excreted in the manure. The pile should also be located a safe distance from any buildings or paddocks, as the heat of decay has been known to result in spontaneous combustion. If you dispose of waste by dumping it in a trash container, the container should be metal with a tight-fitting lid. For protection, keep a water hose or fire extinguisher nearby.

Protecting You and Your Horse with Equine Insurance

Any good riding and boarding stable carries insurance to protect itself against financial losses arising from horse-related accidents. A boarding contract or agreement should spell out the liabilities and responsibilities for both parties so that there are no surprises, in the event that something happens to your horse while in someone else's care.

As a horse owner, you need to be financially protected as well, because you are liable for any injuries or damages your horse causes to other people or property. Many people assume that their homeowner's insurance policy will provide adequate protection, but this is not always the case. You should consult a professional insurance agent to inquire about your coverage needs and options.

There are several types of equine insurance policies, but most important is liability coverage. Make sure you're covered for at least a million dollars, or more if you can afford it. If a lawsuit is brought against you, appropriate liability coverage can help save your home and other assets.

Depending on your financial preparedness, you can also purchase separate coverage for equine medical and surgical expenses, mortality, theft, and loss of use of the horse. If you think buying a dressage horse is expensive, wait until your animal experiences a major illness or injury. During any long-term treatment or recovery, the veterinary bills can mount up fast. Equine medical and surgical policies are available to help you meet such unexpected expenses.

Mortality coverage is like life insurance for your horse. It insures you against the loss of a valuable horse if it dies from disease or injury or if it must be humanely destroyed to relieve incurable suffering. Believe it not, some unscrupulous people have been known to kill their horses to collect insurance money. Therefore, most companies have strict provisions written into their contracts about euthanizing a horse, and they will not pay off unless you adhere to their requirements. If you purchase this type of insurance, make sure you read the contract and understand the requirements.

Loss-of-use insurance is like disability coverage for your horse. It insures against loss in situations when a horse becomes permanently disabled because of disease or injury. The horse may not need to be destroyed, but it can no longer be used for its designated purpose. Most policies require a veterinarian to certify that this is true.

It's important to understand that insurance is designed to protect you against unexpected financial loss and to put you back where you were if such a loss occurs. It isn't meant to pay for every expense that comes along. Horses are generally insured for their current market value, which is usually the purchase price. However, companies will review recent show records, breeding records, and so forth to determine a horse's value.

Of course, regardless of what equine insurance options you choose, your best backup insurance plan is to take full responsibility for your horse's care and safety. Put your horse on a top-notch routine health care program that includes disease and parasite control and stick with it religiously. Even if you're boarding, you should oversee and closely monitor his care, know what he is being fed and how often, know where and when he's turned out, and voice any concerns you may have in a polite, considerate manner.

Keeping Your Horse Healthy

Keeping your horse healthy requires routine vaccinations, parasite control, regular veterinary and dental care, and regular hoof trimming and shoeing services. This means you need to find and establish good relationships with a veterinarian, a farrier, and perhaps even an equine dentist.

Selecting a Veterinarian

Because maintaining good health is of paramount importance for a high-performance dressage horse, one of the most important decisions you'll make as a horse owner is what veterinarian to use. If you board at a stable, the facility probably already has a vet who comes regularly to administer routine immunizations and other services. Veterinarians usually charge a flat fee just for driving to the farm to cover the cost of gas and travel time. This is called the farm visit or farm call fee. Typically, the boarders whose horses are being seen that day split the cost of the farm call fee, which helps hold down your veterinary expenses.

Make an effort to be present when the veterinarian sees your horse, especially the first time. You need to get acquainted with the person who's caring for your horse's health and build a good working relationship.

If you need to find your own veterinarian, ask your riding instructor, other boarders, or horse people in the community to recommend someone. Your local telephone directory lists veterinarians in the yellow pages. You can also check with your local branch of the American Veterinary Medical Association (www.avma.org) or the American Association of Equine Practitioners (www.aaep.org).

Nowadays, most veterinarians who treat horses specialize in equine practice exclusively. There are also veterinarians who specialize in equine dentistry. Regardless of the person you select, make sure you are comfortable with the way he deals with you and your horse.

If you're a first-time horse owner, use the routine visits as an opportunity to ask your veterinarian for advice on horse care and nutrition. Decide whether you feel at ease with the way the doctor addresses your questions and concerns and whether he explains terms, procedures, or findings in a way that you understand.

Find out what number you need to call after hours for emergency services. Post your veterinarian's phone number in a handy place for easy reference. Make sure someone at your barn knows who to call in an emergency if you can't be reached.

As far as maintaining a good relationship with your vet, he'll be very happy if you catch your horse, bring him in from the field, and have him ready and waiting to be seen when the doctor arrives. You may also need to help restrain the horse during the examination. It's also important to express your willingness to listen and learn. Your veterinarian's professional advice and guidance will be a valuable asset to you as a horse owner, so make good use of the time you spend together.

Keeping Up with a Vaccination Program

Establishing a routine health care and vaccination program is one of the most important components of horse management. Start a health record book for your horse and keep track of all inoculation dates, dewormings, dental care, farrier visits, and other health-related issues. Your veterinarian can recommend an appropriate health care schedule and advise you about any particular equine diseases common to the region where you live. Early spring is the time of year when veterinarians typically perform annual checkups, give booster shots, and run a current Coggins test for the upcoming show season.

Generally, horses in the United States are routinely vaccinated for equine influenza, equine encephalomyelitis, tetanus, rabies, and, in most regions now, West Nile virus. Selected animals in certain parts of the country may receive other available vaccines on a timetable recommended by a veterinarian.

Understanding Equine Diseases

As a horse owner, you must keep accurate health records on your horse, you must be able to recognize when the horse is sick and in need of veterinary treatment, and you must be prepared to handle emergencies. Regardless of whether you board or keep your horse at home, his health and veterinary care are always your responsibility, so read, ask questions, and learn as much as you can about equine diseases, immunizations, and health care.

The scope of this book is not intended to cover equine health or nutrition in any depth. Volumes have been written on these topics. See the "References" at the back of this book, where some of the many fine books on the market that specifically address equine health care are listed. Read as many books as you can and buy at least one comprehensive horse health care manual to keep on hand as a reference. Remember, your veterinarian is your best resource for horse health information and advice.

The following is a brief overview of just a few of the more common or well-known equine diseases that every horse owner should be familiar with:

Equine Encephalomyelitis

Several different viruses cause equine encephalomyelitis, also called sleeping sickness. The malady is a mosquito-borne infection that affects the central nervous system, resulting in death in a high percentage of infected horses. The three major types are designated geographically as Venezuelan (VEE), Eastern (EEE), and Western (WEE) encephalomyelitis. In areas with a long mosquito season, vaccination may be recommended more often than once a year.

Equine Infectious Anemia

Also called swamp fever, this disease threatens the world's horse population seriously enough to warrant mandatory testing and strict lifelong quarantine or euthanasia for horses testing positive for it. It is spread by blood, usually via biting insects, such as horse flies and mosquitoes. The disease has no cure, and horses that survive equine infectious anemia (EIA) can become a source of infection to other horses. Some horses can carry the virus and show no apparent symptoms.

The reliable Coggins test, named for the researcher who developed it approximately twenty-five years ago, is used to diagnose or rule out the presence of this contagious disease. A new EIA test, ELISA, produces results more quickly, but the standard Coggins is still considered more accurate. Although regulations and testing intervals vary from region to region, a negative Coggins is required for entry in most U.S. horse shows and for interstate transport of horses. The U.S. Department of Agriculture requires a negative Coggins for horses imported from foreign countries. Any horse that tests positive must be reported to the appropriate authorities.

Equine Influenza

Several types of viruses can cause flu-like symptoms in horses, including high fever, cough, nasal discharge, watery eyes, enlarged lymph nodes, stiff legs, and breathing difficulty. It is spread from horse to horse by coughing and sneezing. Although usually not fatal, sick horses that are being shipped to shows, exposed to bad weather, or stressed in other ways can develop fatal complications, such as pneumonia or inflammation of the heart muscle. Horses that rarely leave the farm may need a flu vaccination only once a year; however, horses that are exposed to other groups of horses that come and go (as at a boarding stable, shows, or trail rides) should be vaccinated more often, on a schedule recommended by a veterinarian.

Rhinopneumonitis

This is another common respiratory ailment in horses, caused by a herpes virus, which can have serious consequences, especially in pregnant mares. Vaccination recommendations are similar to influenza.

Tetanus

This life-threatening disease is caused by bacteria living in the soil that release a toxin, which targets the horse's nervous system. The bacteria typically enter the horse's system via deep puncture wounds. Fortunately, immunity is easily achieved with an initial tetanus shot followed by annual boosters. Commonly called lockjaw, tetanus causes paralysis, muscle rigidity, and respiratory failure, resulting in death in a high percentage of infected horses. To protect your horse, most veterinarians will recommend a tetanus booster in conjunction with any serious wound treatment.

Rabies

Because this viral disease can be transmitted to humans, regular vaccination is a must, even though the incidence of rabies in horses is relatively low. Horses are most often exposed to the rabies virus via the bite of a wild animal, such as a skunk, raccoon, or fox. Although some horse owners choose to administer their own vaccines, it is best to have your veterinarian give the rabies injection because of legal concerns. Should your horse ever bite a human, the authorities can consult the medical records and thereby legally recognize the vaccine. Otherwise, the quarantine requirements may be dire.

Potomac Horse Fever

First recognized in the Potomac valley of Virginia and Maryland in 1979, this infectious disease of the gastrointestinal tract is now found in many other areas of the country. It has a high mortality rate and often starts with depression and loss of appetite and may progress to profuse diarrhea and colic. Laminitis (founder) is a serious complication that can jeopardize the horse's life or future performance career.

Until recently, the vector that spreads the disease was unknown. But research indicates that freshwater snails and the parasites they harbor may be to blame. For this reason, it's preferable to water horses from troughs, instead of ponds, streams, and other aquatic habitats where these snails may dwell. Vaccination is also recommended if you live in any area where the disease has surfaced.

Strangles

This upper respiratory tract infection is characterized by enlarged and abscessed lymph nodes of the jaws. The disease is highly contagious among horses via infected nasal secretions. A vaccine is available, but it has some risks, and its effectiveness is controversial. For this reason, not all veterinarians recommend it routinely.

West Nile Virus

This mosquito-borne viral disease was first detected in the eastern United States in 1999 and has since marched westward to become one of the fastest growing threats to horses. The virus, which causes encephalitis, or swelling of the brain and spinal cord, and related neurologic symptoms, has also been found in Africa, Asia, the Middle East, and the Mediterranean region of

Europe. Mosquitoes acquire the West Nile virus from birds and pass it on to other birds, animals, and people. Migrating birds appear to play a role in the spread of the disease, because they can travel great distances in a short time.

Symptoms may include stumbling or tripping, wandering or circling, partial paralysis, appetite loss, head tilt, walking into objects, muscle incoordination, fever, convulsions, or coma. While humans and horses may be infected by the virus, there is no documentation that infected horses can spread the virus to uninfected horses, humans, or other animals.

Since a vaccine became available in 2000, studies indicate that most cases of West Nile virus occur in unvaccinated horses. Therefore, horses can be protected by adhering to a vaccination regimen with annual boosters and by effective mosquito-control methods. Horses that travel and compete in areas that have a heavy mosquito season may require more frequent boosters, so consult your veterinarian for the appropriate recommendations for your area and circumstances.

Equine Protozoal Myeloencephalitis

Also a neurological disease that attacks the central nervous system and causes inflammation of the brain and spinal cord, equine protozoal myeloencephalitis (EPM) symptoms are often confused with West Nile virus. Only a veterinarian can distinguish the two with appropriate testing, but one clue is that EPM tends to affect one side of the horse more than the other.

EPM is caused by an organism called a protozoan. It is transmitted to the horse by the opossum, which is how the illness came to be called the Possum disease. Racehorses and show horses tend to be at higher risk than breeding and pleasure horses, possibly because stress plays a role in the disease development.

Treatment is expensive, often lasting several months, and relapses are common. A vaccine has been developed, but its efficacy and potency are still being tested. Ask your veterinarian about vaccine availability and protocol.

Disorders of Dietary Origin

Although there are several disorders of dietary origin in the horse, the following two are the ones horse owners need to be especially aware of, as they are fairly common, potentially life-threatening, and constitute a true medical emergency.

Colic

Although not a specific disease, colic is a general term applied to digestive upset in the horse characterized by abdominal pain. Causes may include overfeeding, sudden change in feed, eating moldy or unfit feed, improperly chewed feed, or parasite infestation. There are several types of colic, including spasmodic colic (the most common type), impaction colic (in which a portion of the bowel becomes obstructed), and intussusception (in which a loop of intestine telescopes inside itself).

Horses cannot vomit and, therefore, cannot rid themselves of stomach matter that may be churning within and causing an upset. That's why the owner must be especially vigilant for signs of colic and initiate veterinary treatment right away. Common symptoms include:

- Biting at the flanks
- Kicking at the belly
- Frequent lying down and rolling
- Abnormal sweating
- Unusual stance

Colic can be mild or severe, but any sign of abdominal discomfort in the horse is cause for concern and should be checked out by a veterinarian without delay. The condition can sometimes be fatal or require surgery to save the horse's life. Prevention includes good horse management and careful attention to feeding practices.

Laminitis (Founder)

This noninfectious inflammation of the sensitive, inner connective tissues of the hoof, called the laminae, can be extremely painful and potentially crippling. (See the figure on this page for a look at a horse's hoof.) The laminae layer holds a small foot bone, called the coffin bone, in place, but when the tissues become inflamed, the bone may rotate and separate from the rest of the hoof. In severe cases, the displaced bone can even pierce the sole of the foot, necessitating the humane destruction of the horse.

Causes may include overeating, digestive disturbances, too lush pastures (especially in spring when the grass first turns green), retained afterbirth, foot concussion, certain disease processes, and sometimes even certain medications. Founder is more common in the front feet, but can occur in all four. The condition is always considered serious, as it can result in permanent lameness or death.

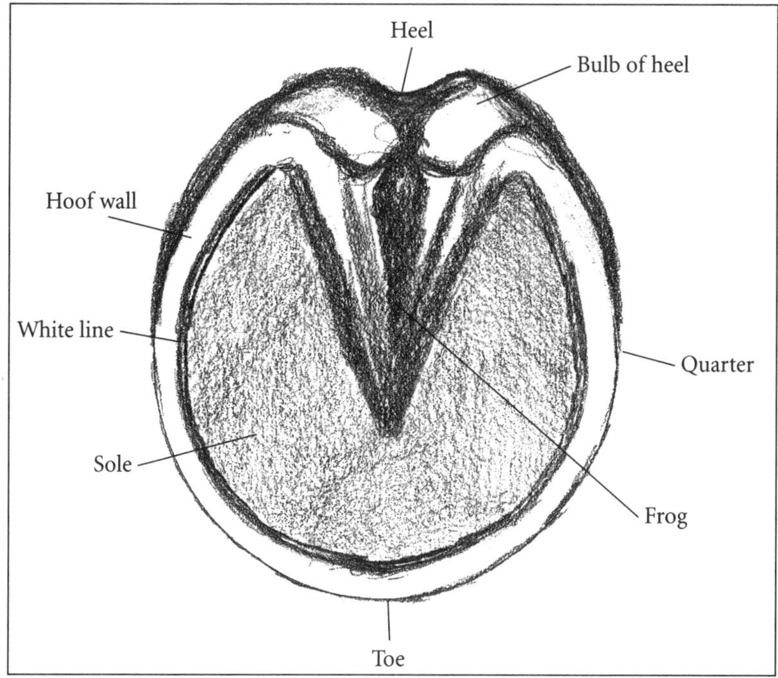

The structures of the horse's hoof.

Common symptoms include:

- Marked lameness
- Marked tenderness of the feet
- Unwillingness to move
- Unusual stance (forefeet planted out in front with weight rocked back on the hind end)

Contact your veterinarian right away if your horse displays any of these symptoms. Immediate treatment may help lessen the damage. As with colic, prevention includes good horse management and careful attention to feeding practices, including feeding the proper amount.

Ulcers

Gastric ulcers have only recently been recognized as a health problem in horses. They seem to be most common in horses that lead stressful lives, such as show horses and racehorses. In the past, the condition was frequently misdiagnosed because of the varied and often vague symptoms of unease and discomfort. These may include poor appetite, poor coat, restlessness, ill temper, reluctance to work under saddle, and chronic colic.

According to traditional thinking, the way we feed horses today possibly contributes to the formation of gastric ulcers. Under natural conditions, horses graze most of the day, so their stomach always has something in it to absorb the acids produced during the digestive process. However, stabled horses fed two large meals a day go for several hours in between with an empty stomach. The acids keep churning and eventually eat away at the stomach lining, causing an ulcer.

Treatment can be expensive and involves using drugs that inhibit gastric acid secretion. Prevention is much cheaper. Feed the same amounts, but in smaller, more frequent meals. Likewise, spread smaller hay portions throughout the day so your horse always has something to nibble on. Allow your horse ample turnout and grazing time in a pasture. If he's in intensive training for competition, give him a regular day off to relax.

Avoiding Internal Parasites

A parasite is an organism that lives in or on another host organism. Horses can be host to many different kinds of parasites and require a regular deworming program to keep them free of serious infestations. They acquire parasites naturally by grazing, as the life cycle of many worms is completed in or on the ground. By confining our animals to small grazing areas, we compound their chances of exposure. Weight loss or a potbelly, poor coat quality, tail rubbing, diarrhea, and anemia can be signs that parasitic infection has taken a stronghold inside the horse.

A heavy load of internal parasites can have serious health consequences. Aside from jeopardizing a horse's overall vigor and nutrition, parasite infestation ranks high among the most common causes of colic, as many species migrate through the intestines, causing damage or obstructions along the way.

Common Types of Internal Parasites

The following are common types of internal parasites that infect horses.

- **Large and small strongyles:** Blood-sucking parasites that grow in the intestines of the horse, causing damage to the blood vessels, the digestive tract, and other vital organs.
- **Ascarids:** Roundworms that live in the small intestines. More common in foals and young horses, these parasites can cause coughing, inflammation, and other problems in the gut.
- **Bots:** The bot fly lays its eggs on the hair of the horse's legs, shoulders, or jaws. The eggs appear as tiny yellow specks on the hair tips. When they hatch, the larvae migrate toward the mouth and eventually end up being swallowed. They live in the horse's stomach for many

months before passing out in the manure, burrowing into the ground and later emerging as adult bot flies to begin the cycle anew. The entire transformation requires about a year.

- **Tapeworms:** Until recently, tapeworms were not thought to be problematic in the horse. However, research reveals a connection between tapeworms and several types of colic.

Parasite Control

A good parasite control program starts with having your veterinarian analyze a sample of your horse's manure to determine what parasites are present in the gut. Your veterinarian will then tailor an appropriate deworming strategy, advise you on what products to use, and how often to use them. Nowadays, medicated paste dewormers, such as ivermectin or oxibendazole, are easy to administer and readily available over the counter at tack and feed stores. But to be effective, any deworming medication must be administered based on the type of parasites present and their life cycle stage.

Different dewormers destroy different types of parasites at certain stages of development, so that's why it's important to consult a veterinarian first to make sure you're using the right deworming agent for the right worm. Because horsekeeping situations and individual horses differ, and because parasite exposure varies significantly from region to region, you should never select an over-the-counter broad-spectrum dewormer and administer it willy-nilly without first finding out what kind of parasites you're trying to kill.

Always read labels carefully to make sure you're administering the agent properly and using the correct dosage. For example, it's important to determine your horse's weight and administer the dose accordingly. A girth measuring tape will give you a close approximation of weight. Your veterinarian can show you how to give the correct amount.

It's also important to rotate the type or chemical class of dewormers you use, because some parasites may build up a resistance to one that's used over and over again. Rotation may be accomplished by changing drug classes annually or every time you deworm, depending on your veterinarian's recommendations.

To prevent recontamination, all horses on a property should be on the same deworming schedule. Also, periodic deworming must be combined with cleanliness in the stable and good pasture management. This involves removing manure to reduce the number of infective larvae in the environment and giving some grazing areas a periodic "rest" from horses, so that the parasites can die off.

Keeping Up with Hoof Care

Without good feet, your horse cannot carry you far in any dressage test. Aside from your veterinarian, your farrier (a person who shoes horses) is the next most important person in your lineup of equine health care professionals. In bygone days, farriers were called blacksmiths, because they often forged ironwork other than horseshoes.

Most horses that are shown or ridden regularly need to wear metal shoes. Horseshoes help protect the feet from cracking, splitting, and excessive wear. Many owners shoe only the front feet, rather than all four. This has two advantages: it's less expensive and it's somewhat safer if the horse will be turned out with other horses. Horses often kick at each other, and an unshod foot makes less of an impact than a metal shoe striking bone.

Because a horse's hooves grow just like your hair grows, the shoes need to be reset or replaced every four to eight weeks, and the foot must be trimmed back to preserve a proper angle to the ground. Even if you opt to let your horse go barefoot, without shoes, his feet will need to be trimmed once a month or so, depending on how fast his hooves grow.

Selecting a Farrier

If you board at a stable, the facility probably uses a regular farrier, who comes on a set schedule and shoes several horses at one time. If you need to select your own farrier, ask your veterinarian and other dressage people for recommendations. Some farriers specialize in corrective shoeing, or in shoeing horses used in a particular discipline, such as jumping or gaited horses. So make certain you find one familiar with the demands of dressage work.

From time to time, a horse will throw a shoe. When this happens, call your farrier right away, and do not ride the horse until the shoe is replaced. Try to select a farrier who lives close enough by to come out fairly quickly when such situations arise. A thrown shoe always seems to occur at the most inconvenient times, such as the day of your dressage show. Often, the larger horse shows will have a farrier on the grounds.

Routine Hoof Care

Aside from regular shoeing and trimming, the horse's hooves need to be picked out daily and before and after each ride. This gives you a chance to inspect the feet for cracks and other problems and helps ensure that no gravel or stone has become lodged in the hoof that could cause the horse to go lame. The tool for this chore is a hoof pick.

Two or three times a week, you also should brush on a commercial hoof preparation that is formulated to help keep the hoof in good condition. Several varieties of these products are available at tack and feed stores. Ask your farrier what type he recommends for your horse.

Common Foot Problems

Cracks and thrush are two conditions easily spotted during a routine hoof inspection. Abscesses of the foot generally bring on sudden and acute lameness and typically resolve just as quickly once the pressure from the infection inside the foot is released.

- **Cracks:** Most commonly seen are toe, quarter, and heel cracks. Depending on their depth and severity, some hoof cracks can make a horse quite sore, while others cause little or no problem at all. A good farrier studies each individual crack to determine the best way to treat it. Until the cracked area grows out, treatment is often aimed at sealing or otherwise preventing the crack from spreading during foot action.

- **Thrush:** Thrush is a smelly, bacterial infection of the foot that can take hold if the horse is forced to stand in damp, unclean conditions, such as soiled bedding, for a lengthy time. The condition is easy to spot by its foul odor and by a black discharge and soft, flaky matter that scrapes off the sole when the hoof is picked out. Left untreated, the infection can progress and lead to serious lameness. Fortunately, thrush is relatively easy to treat with over-the-counter thrush preparations available at tack and feed stores.
- **Hoof abscesses:** If your horse appears fine one day and is suddenly limping around on three legs the next, suspect a hoof abscess. Abscesses are bacterial infections that arise from various causes, such as gravel, bruise, or puncture wound. Prolonged periods of wet weather, alternating with short dry spells, also tend to increase the incidence of abscesses in pastured horses. An abscess typically starts at the sole of the foot and works up through the hoof wall, often breaking out at the coronary band, where the infection drains. A veterinarian can open the abscess and allow it to drain, which usually provides immediate pain relief to the horse. The affected foot must be soaked periodically in warm water and Epsom salts to continue drawing out the infection. The veterinarian may also prescribe antibiotic or anti-inflammatory drugs, depending on the nature of the injury.

Dental Care

When a horse has dental problems, it may become difficult to bridle or keep on the bit. The horse may toss his head, fidget, or misbehave while being ridden because the bit further irritates an already sore mouth. A sore mouth or badly worn teeth can also affect a horse's ability to chew his food, causing him to lose weight and overall body condition. This problem is more commonly seen in older horses, but can occur at any age.

A horse's teeth continue to grow throughout his lifetime, thereby ensuring that he will have enough enamel left for grazing into old age. And just as an older horse's health care needs change over the years from that of a younger horse, so does his dental care needs.

A horse grinds his food by moving the jaws from side to side. Sometimes this action results in uneven wear as the teeth continue to grow, making it necessary for your veterinarian to file down sharp points that develop on the tooth surfaces. This process, called floating the teeth, generally should be done once a year.

These days, many regions support veterinarians who specialize exclusively in equine dentistry. These docs travel around from barn to barn, armed with power tools, grinding and treating all sorts of dental woes in horses. Because a comfortable, healthy mouth is essential for the dressage horse, who must be ridden into the bridle and on the bit, a yearly check up or two from one of these specialists, if available in your area, is a good investment toward your training and competition goals.

Feeding Your Dressage Horse

The best dressage training and riding in the world won't do your horse a bit of good unless you feed him right. Horses evolved to be grazing animals. Good-quality pasture or hay, a little grain, a salt block, and ample fresh water generally provide adequate nutrition for many mature, casually ridden pleasure mounts. However, exercise and growth increase energy and nutrient needs so that hard-working performance horses, growing foals, and nursing mares typically need some additional feed, vitamins, and minerals.

The scope of this book does not permit detailed coverage of equine nutrition; however, many fine, in-depth volumes exist on the subject. Every responsible horse owner should read and become educated about the different types of hay, grain-based concentrates, and supplements available. Your veterinarian is also a good source of information, as he can best assess your horse's health and body condition and recommend any necessary dietary changes. Any changes in diet should be made gradually.

The way you feed your horse will depend on his individual nutritional needs, on the climatic conditions where you live, and on how often your horse is ridden and worked. In addition, the change of seasons may dictate that you adjust your feeding regimen periodically during the year. For example, if you are fortunate enough to live in an area where grass remains plentiful from spring through autumn, your horse may thrive on just pasture for several months out of the year. You may need to add hay and grain only after the grass begins to die back as colder weather approaches. Similarly, you'll probably need to cut back on your horse's feed a bit, particularly grain, whenever he takes a layoff from his training and showing schedule. He won't need as many calories to burn while he's on vacation.

Because horses are grazing animals, they are designed to eat throughout the day. Therefore, feeding them several small meals a day, rather than two large meals, is closer to the natural state, if they can't be turned out to pasture to graze. Small, frequent feedings also seem to be better for their digestive systems.

Forage and Commercial Feeds

The greatest part of the horse's diet needs to be hay or pasture, called forage. The fiber and roughage is vital to keeping things moving through all those miles of intestines inside. Hay comes in two basic types: legume or grass hay. Legume hay, such as alfalfa, typically has a higher energy and nutrient content than grass hays, such as timothy. Some horsemen prefer one type over the other, while others will feed a mixture of the two. However, the fact that legume hay has a higher protein content must be considered in the balance of the overall ration plan.

Hay is available in bales and cubes and in varying quality and consistency, depending on the region where you live, the weather conditions there, and on the time of year. Good hay should be free of weeds and insects and should not show any signs of mold or dampness. Eating moldy hay can make a horse very sick. Again, check with your veterinarian or the local dressage people in your region to find out what type of hay they usually feed and who their supplier is. Your state extension office can also provide a list of the types of hays most common in your area. Regardless of the type of hay you select, your money will go further if you purchase good-quality hay.

In the growing season months, hay and pasture alone are often fine for a lightly ridden pleasure horse, but they usually will not provide sufficient energy for a hard-working dressage horse. Supplement his forage with a suitably balanced commercial feed containing grains, such as oats, corn, or barley, to provide the extra energy he needs. Sweet feed mixes several grains with a molasses-like syrup to make it palatable to horses, however, the high sugar content can make some horses more high strung. Take care not to overfeed your horse on concentrates. Grain overload and overfeeding or improper feeding in general can lead to colic and laminitis (founder).

Here are some general feeding tips to follow:

- Measure feeds by weight, not volume.
- Feed in tubs, buckets, or mangers that have no sharp corners and that are large enough for the horse to get his nose to the bottom.
- Feed hay below the horse's head height, on the ground or stall floor, to mimic the normal grazing posture.
- If feeding hay to several horses in a field, spread the hay out in several piles, so that everyone gets a chance to eat without having to fight or compete for the food.
- Make sure the horse always has plenty of fresh, clean water to drink.

Nutritional needs change as a horse ages and progresses through various life stages. Foals (baby horses) and nursing mares need more energy and nutrients for growth and reproductive stages. Pregnant mares should not be fed fescue hay or allowed to graze in pastures where fescue grows during their later months of pregnancy. The plant contains a mycotoxin that can cause mares to deliver weak or dead foals. Senior horses, age 20 or older, may need to be fed softer foods that are easier to digest, particularly if their teeth are worn down and they have trouble chewing. Periodically review your feeding plan with your veterinarian during routine visits and ask if any changes need to be made. Always make any feeding changes gradually, so as not to upset the horse's delicate digestive system.

Supplements

Supplements exist in the horse market to enhance or improve practically everything you can think of, from hoof growth to coat sheen. However, most well-fed horses don't need their feed supplemented with extra vitamins and minerals. Besides, too much of a good thing can actually be harmful. Oversupplementing foals, for example, can interfere with the natural growth processes of the bones, muscles, and connective tissues and lead to big problems later on down the road.

There are, however, instances when supplementation may be necessary. For instance, if your horse is aging and not able to digest his nutrients as well as he used to, he may need supplementation, especially if he begins to lose condition. Pregnant and nursing mares generally require some supplementation, as recommended by a veterinarian, to meet the increased demands of reproduction. Horses on poor-quality pasture may also need supplements. But if your horse maintains his body weight and condition well on what you're feeding him, don't try to fix what isn't broken. If you do think your horse may need supplements, seek your veterinarian's advice first.

Aside from nutritional supplements, there are also many joint supplements on the market for horses. Products containing glucosamine and chondroitin have been used for years in performance horses to help maintain the flexibility in their hocks and ease arthritic changes associated with normal aging. Yet, they remain somewhat controversial simply because of the lack of definitive research on their effectiveness. Still, there are many horse owners (myself included) using these products who swear by them and who are convinced that they help.

Because the dressage horse's engine is in the back end, where he drives himself forward from the hindquarters, his hocks bear a lot of weight and suffer a lot of wear and tear over the years. The hock joint is where many a dressage horse experiences stiffness or soundness problems.

While research suggests that joint supplements may help, the buyer must be aware that not all joint supplements are created equal. Much depends on the quality and concentration of ingredients. Even though many brands are expensive, price is no indication of quality or results, and the labels can be misleading. The amounts of glucosamine and chondroitin also vary widely from product to product. This is because the industry has no clear-cut standards or regulations that govern how much is good or how much is too much. There are some good products out there, but here again, you should consult your veterinarian for advice before deciding on one.

Chapter Seven

Buying Tack and Riding Apparel

Dressing for Dressage

Acquiring *tack*—all the stuff you need to ride horses—is one of your largest expenses in the equine hobby, next to the purchase price of your horse. For starters, you'll need a saddle, saddle pads, bridle, bits, stirrups, a halter, lead ropes, a riding whip, a longe whip, a longe line, blanket, cooler, and an assortment of grooming brushes, curry comb, hoof pick, and related horse care items. Then, of course, you'll need riding clothes. The list will grow the longer you're in the sport. And every time you travel to a show, the town's tack store will be one of the highlights of your visit, as you seek out that something new and different that you don't really need but can't possibly live without.

Saddles

When selecting tack, look for quality items that will last and service you for many years. For dressage competitions, an English saddle and bridle are required. In the lower levels, either an all-purpose saddle or a dressage saddle with stirrups is acceptable. For Federation Equestre Internationale (FEI) level tests, a dressage saddle is mandatory.

The dressage saddle is designed with a longer, straighter flap panel to accommodate the longer leg position used in the discipline.

It has a deep seat that helps balance the rider's upright position in the center. The stirrup bar is also set slightly farther back to assist the rider's position.

The saddle may be black or brown. Choose the hue that best complements the color of your horse. Prices range from several hundred to several thousands of dollars, depending on the brand and quality. Most serious competitors purchase a high-end saddle for show use only and reserve a less expensive model for everyday schooling.

If you aren't ready to shell out a couple of grand for a leather saddle or two, try a synthetic. Today's synthetic saddles have the appearance of leather, are durable, lightweight, easy to clean, reasonably priced, and ideal for people just starting out in dressage. They are acceptable in lower-level competition and ideal for schooling. Plus, you don't have to fuss with all the extra maintenance leather requires. Later, if you decide to continue moving up the levels in dressage, you'll probably want to purchase a more expensive leather model for show and retain your synthetic for schooling.

Saddle Fit

The most important selection issue regarding any saddle is the fit. It must fit both horse and rider well. If the saddle doesn't fit you, the rider, well, it can't do a good job of supporting your position on the horse. You may find yourself constantly fighting against your own body, trying to readjust and maintain a correct seat in a saddle that's too big or too small.

If the saddle doesn't fit the horse well, your horse may develop saddle sores or a tender, bruised back. Sometimes, behavioral problems arise from being ridden in poorly fitting tack, as the horse protests against the constant discomfort. If the pain becomes severe enough, he may even seek to unload his rider at any given opportunity. A sore back will also negatively impact your horse's way of going and performance ability. If he's hurting from an ill-fitting saddle, there's no way can he relax, stretch his top line, and round his back, the way a good dressage horse is supposed to do.

Many people do not realize that the fit of a saddle may also change over time as the flocking inside its panels packs down, or as the horse loses or gains weight or muscle mass. For this reason, you should have the saddle fit assessed by a professional saddle fitter every other year or so. A saddle fitter can remove or replenish the flocking as needed and can also recommend appropriate pads to use.

Younger dressage horses in particular tend to develop more muscle as they become better fit and conditioned to performing their gymnastic maneuvers. This can affect the saddle fit. In addition, if you acquire a different horse during your riding career, you likely will also have to change saddles to ensure a proper fit on the new mount.

One way to figure out what saddle width will fit your horse is to bend a wire coat hanger over the withers. Then take the bent wire to your tack store or trace the arch on a piece of paper. The best way to fit a saddle, however, is to simply try it out on the horse and ride in it. Some tack shops will allow you to do this, as long as you tape or wrap the stirrup leathers in socks to prevent scratching or marring the new leather.

As you look at the saddle from front and back, you should be able to see daylight underneath the gullet with a rider's weight. That is, there should be a gap underneath from front to back that comfortably clears the horse's back. The front arch of the saddle, called the pommel, should not press down on the horse's withers when a rider is aboard.

A well-fitting saddle fits securely and spreads the rider's weight evenly over the horse's back, keeping pressure away from the spine. If the gullet presses down on the horse's spine at any point or if the saddle pinches, the horse will eventually become pressure sore at that spot. The seat of the saddle should be level at its center, neither too high in front nor too low in back, or vice versa.

Saddle Pads

Most dressage riders prefer square, white pads, and this is what you'll usually see at schooling and recognized shows, although their use is optional. Sometimes you'll see a gray horse ridden with a black pad. Or you'll see white pads trimmed with a colored braid or border. Upper-level riders often use swallow-tail pads that flare out in the back, creating an elegant look and providing a clean and contrasting resting place for the rider's dark coat tails.

When the horse is saddled, the saddle pad should be tucked up into the gullet from front to back. This prevents the edges of the pad from pressing down across the horse's withers or back and rubbing him or creating pressure points.

When you unsaddle, look at the dirty sweat marks on the underside of the pad. If the marks are even down both shoulders and across the back, the saddle is distributing the rider's weight evenly. If the marks are uneven, you may need to adjust your saddle fit. Uneven marks can also be a telltale sign that the rider is sitting unevenly, for example, with his weight more to one side than the other.

The rider is permitted to display a logo or sponsor name on the saddle pad in competition. The U.S. Equestrian Federation (USEF) *Rule Book* specifies the size and placement of such advertisement and should be adhered to accordingly.

Girths

The typical dressage saddle has longer girth straps to allow use of either a short- or normal-length girth, as desired. The advantage of a short girth is that it buckles lower down on the horse's belly, reducing the bulk under the rider's leg.

The girth can be leather or synthetic with double buckles on both ends and should match or complement the color of the saddle. If one end is elasticized, the girth is easier to fasten around a big-barreled horse or a puffer—one that puffs up with air to evade the tightening girth. The elasticized end is buckled on the near side of the horse.

For the horse's comfort, tighten the girth gently and gradually. You should be able to insert two fingers between the girth and the horse's side. Many horses acquire the habit of blowing up with air while being saddled and then letting it out after they start moving.

It's amazing how much air they can suck in and how long they can hold it that way. A girth that at first seems tight can become dangerously loose after the horse gets under way and expels some air. So check the girth once before you mount, and again after you mount and have walked around a few minutes during warm-up.

Horses that have ultrasensitive skin may benefit from the added protection of a sheepskin or fake fur girth sleeve that prevents chaffing and rubbing in the girth area. Girth galls or sores can render a horse unfit to ride until the sores have time to heal.

Stirrups and Stirrup Leathers

With English-type saddles, the stirrup irons, stirrup leathers, and stirrup treads are generally all sold separately; whereas with western saddles the stirrups are typically attached. This often comes as a surprise to some western riders crossing over to dressage to improve their reining technique. (The sport of reining is sometimes considered the western discipline's closest equivalent to a dressage test, as similar principles apply.)

The stirrup irons (called irons even though they are crafted of stainless steel today instead of iron), are the metal part that your foot rests on. For safety reasons, the iron must fit the rider's foot with about half an inch on either side of the boot. To check the fit, place the stirrup upright on the floor and stand in it with the ball of your foot (wearing riding boots) resting on the iron. Next, have someone hold the iron in place while you rock back on your heel. Your toe should clear the top arch, as should happen if you were to fall from the horse. If the stirrup does not fit properly, the rider risks getting his foot caught and being dragged during a spill.

Alternatively, the rider may choose safety stirrups, which are recommended for children and beginning adult riders, as well as for more accomplished riders who are getting on green horses. The safety stirrup has a tight-fitting rubber or elastic strap on one side that breaks away if the rider's foot gets caught during a fall. The strap is placed on the outside edge of the iron.

When not mounted, run the stirrup irons up the leathers and tuck the leathers through as shown here.

Stirrup treads are the rubber inserts that fit into the footplate. They provide extra grip and can help prevent the rider's foot from slipping out of the stirrup, especially during damp weather.

Stirrup leathers may be real leather or a durable synthetic material that looks like leather. Regardless of what they're made of, stirrup leathers are a vital part of your riding safety and should be well maintained and inspected periodically for cracks, loose stitching, and other weaknesses. When in doubt, replace suspect leathers with new ones.

The stirrup leathers attach to the stirrup bars under the saddle skirt. For added safety, the stirrup bars are open on the ends. If the rider falls and gets a foot hung in the stirrup, her dangling weight will yank the leathers off the bars. Some stirrup bars can be opened or closed on the ends, but you should never ride with them closed.

When leading a saddled horse, always run the irons up the leathers and tuck the leathers through to avoid snagging on any object. (See the figure on this page.) Flapping irons banging against the sides may spook a green or sensitive horse, possibly causing him to bolt.

Bridles and Bits

Competition rules require a plain snaffle bridle for Introductory through Second Level tests. Third and Fourth Levels may use a snaffle bridle or a double bridle, and FEI levels use the double bridle. You should school your horse in the required equipment for your level of competition, although you may wish to have a second bridle that matches your saddle color set aside for show purposes.

The Snaffle Bridle

The snaffle bridle has a single rein attached to a smooth snaffle bit, as shown in the figure on this page. There are several varieties of snaffle bits, but not all are permitted in dressage. The USEF *Rule Book* describes and displays illustrations of the ones currently allowed. If you are in doubt whether a bit is correct for dressage, compare it to the *Rule Book* pictures and read the descriptions. Wire and twisted snaffles are not permitted. Ring stewards may inspect bits and other saddlery at a show, so make sure you have correct equipment and that it is properly worn and adjusted. Wearing the wrong equipment can get you disqualified, and ignorance is never an acceptable excuse.

Snaffle bridles are most commonly outfitted with a regular cavesson noseband (see the figure on page 168), a flash noseband (also shown on page 168), or a dropped noseband. The rules also permit crossed and padded nosebands in the lower levels. Double bridles use a regular cavesson. Each type of noseband acts differently on the horse's mouth, but generally speaking, they all put

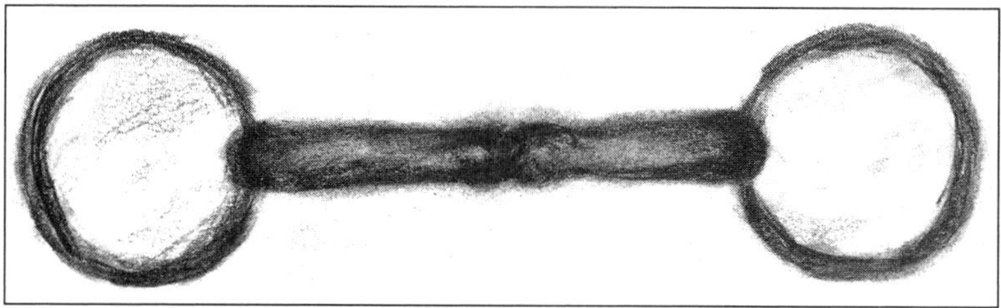

Ordinary snaffle bit with single-jointed mouthpiece.

Cavesson noseband.

Flash noseband.

pressure on the nose or mouth area to help keep the bit in the horse's mouth and the mouth shut. You should familiarize yourself with how each piece of equipment functions. For example, the dropped noseband fastens below the bit and, when fitted correctly, effectively discourages the horse from opening his mouth to evade the bit.

The flash noseband is really a regular cavesson with a detachable piece that functions much like a dropped noseband. In other disciplines, the flash noseband has the advantage of allowing a standing martingale to be attached to the cavesson; however, martingales are not permitted in dressage tests. Discuss with your trainer or instructor which type of equipment works best on your horse and why.

The Double Bridle

A double bridle uses two bits, a light snaffle and curb, and two reins. When used on a double bridle, a snaffle bit is called a bridoon, and it is often somewhat smaller and thinner than the typical bit used on a plain snaffle bridle. This is because two bits are going in the mouth, so it has to be a little smaller to make room for both. Again, the competition rules permit only certain types of bridoons and curb bits (on the next page) for use on double bridles.

Riding in a double bridle requires a great deal of practice and precision to use correctly. That's why you see it only at the higher levels. It is not a device for the novice. The curb bit acts on the mouth differently than the snaffle, exerting leverage on the bars of the horse's mouth, the chin, and the poll. This combined action causes the horse to lower his head, tuck in his nose, and flex at the poll, an effect that helps achieve greater roundness and collection.

The snaffle bit exerts no such leverage, but it is very direct in its action nonetheless. The snaffle exerts pressure primarily on the tongue, lips, and the bars of the mouth. Thus, the effect of the bit varies with the type of mouthpiece it has—whether jointed or solid—and whether it has rings or straight cheeks. For

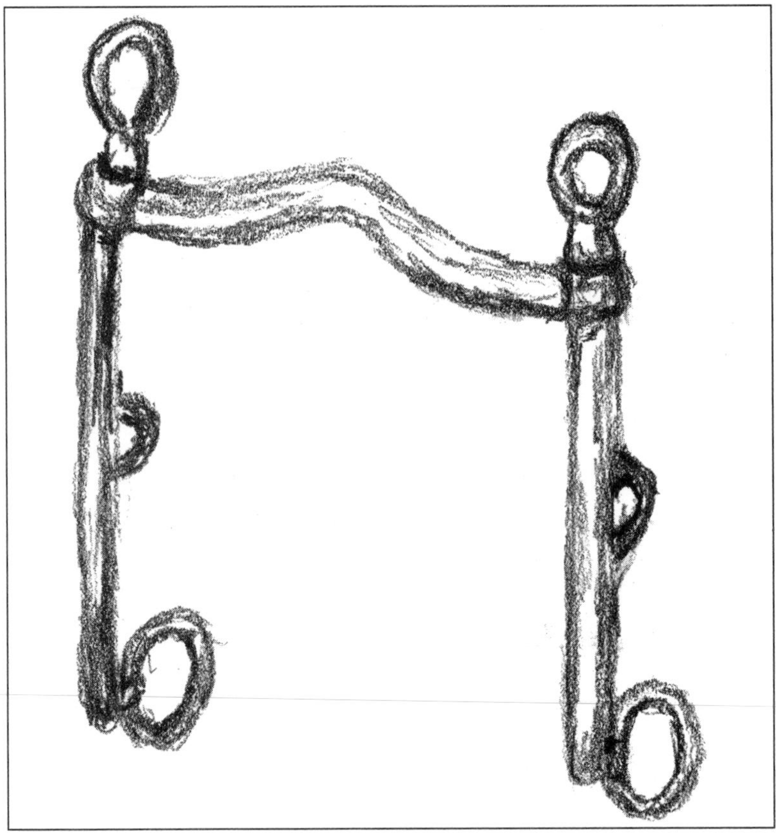

Curb bit. The hump in the middle is called a port.

example, the full-cheek snaffle has long cheek pieces that put pressure on the horse's cheeks. This extra action is useful if the horse is difficult to bend or turn, for example. Plus, the cheek pieces prevent the bit from being pulled through the horse's mouth.

Despite the purposes intended for the various designs, however, it's important to remember that the type of bit or bridle you use, or any piece of tack for that matter, is not going to make you a better rider of its own accord. Some people have the misconception that if they throw a double bridle on the horse and haul on the reins real hard so that the horse's nose comes in, they've achieved collection.

Not so. You can't collect a horse from the front end, with just your hands. Collection comes from behind, from your legs and seat driving the horse forward from the hindquarters into the bridle, and then sculpting that roundness with a measured degree of rein contact. When truly collected, the dressage horse feels light and responsive in the bridle and forefront. This level of the art is not something that can be achieved by heavy-handedness. Only careful training and progressive conditioning will get you there. Resorting to fancy gadgets to hold a horse in a frame won't yield genuine results. Remember, there are no short cuts in dressage. Selecting appropriate tack and training aids for your horse's stage of development will help you reach the desired results, when used correctly, but ultimately, you, as rider and trainer, must understand what you are doing and why each step of the way.

Riding Apparel

Basically, the rider's gear consists of boots, a safety helmet, riding breeches, shirt, jacket, and gloves. Riding apparel adheres to long-standing traditions and seems stilted to many modern-day observers, but every item serves a purpose. For example, the tie and stock pin commonly seen in show attire could be used in the field to fashion a temporary sling for a rider's broken arm.

Show-Ring Attire

Dress required for competition depends on the level at which you are showing and the type of show you are entering. The dress code for schooling shows is more lenient than for recognized shows. At a recognized show, you can be eliminated for a dress code violation.

Upper-level riders wear the traditional and elegant shadbelly coats with tails. For Training through Fourth Levels, all you need is a short riding coat of conservative color, usually black or brown. White or light-colored breeches are the norm, as is a traditional white shirt, worn with a tie, choker, or stock tie. Although there are no written rules for Introductory Level attire, most riders adhere to Training Level requirements. The nicer you look in front of the judges, the better; see the figure on page 173.

A hat always tops off the outfit at a show. For the lower levels, velvet hunt caps or bowlers (also called derbies) are standard choices. Upper-level riders must wear a top hat when wearing a shadbelly coat (has tailcoats) and a derby if sporting a short jacket. Hats do not need to be safety-approved; however, any rider may choose to wear protective headgear, preferably with a clear chin harness, without penalty.

Dress Boots

Most riders at the lower levels choose tall, black leather dress boots for show because they look sharp, but brown boots, field boots, zippered boots, and even rubber boots are allowed. The FEI levels specify black dress boots only.

Tall leather boots protect the rider's legs from the forces of friction against the saddle and stirrup leathers, as well as high brush in the field. For schooling, many riders opt for short paddock boots, which are easier to fit and pull on and off. Tall boots do a better job of helping to stabilize the legs against the horse, but they are more expensive and more difficult to fit, especially for riders with large calves, and often must be custom-made.

Getting them on and off also requires you to be a bit of a contortionist at times. Unless they fit your leg loosely, which they shouldn't, you need a pair of boot pulls to get them on and a boot jack or a good strong tug from an assistant to get them off. For everyday use, you can simplify this a little if you take your boots to a leather shop and have zippers or a piece of stretch elastic material called a gusset inserted along the back seam or on the inside calf.

It took me awhile to get used to wearing tall boots, as they have a long break-in period and can really raise some blisters when they're new. But now I prefer the superior comfort and protection they offer my leg over the short jodhpur boots. I normally school in tall field boots (these lace up at the ankle) and reserve my custom-made dress boots for shows and special occasions.

This rider is neatly attired for lower-level competition.

If you care for your boots properly, they should give you many years of service. Wipe the hair, dirt, and sweat off them after every ride and store them clean in a boot bag. Insert boot trees or rolled up newspapers inside each boot to help them retain their standing shape. Polish and condition the leather periodically with one of many products available on the market made specifically for the care of riding boots. If you use the same pair of boots for show and everyday riding, as many people do, you'll need to take especially good care of them to keep them looking nice. Ask your local tack shop to recommend good boot care products.

Riding Pants

White breeches are the norm for show dress, but hardly practical for everyday riding. So buy a white pair or two and put them aside for show. If you're going to a show that is two days or longer, you'll probably need a clean pair for each day, or for each class, because white gets dirty very easily. For schooling, choose any other colors you like. Your riding instructor will be able to see your hips and posture more clearly against the saddle if you wear a lighter, contrasting color, such as light gray or tan. Buy several pairs of riding pants for everyday use, as they get dirty and wear out quickly, especially in the crotch and seat.

To minimize chaffing from the friction against the saddle, riding pants are reinforced along the inside knee and leg, and sometimes in the seat. However, this extra reinforcement in the breeches doesn't always provide enough protection for the sensitive skin underneath. Many riders still feel themselves smarting in the groin area after only a short workout. And saddle sores can make life miserable for several days! A gel pad or padded sheepskin seat-saver that covers the saddle during schooling sessions may help. An advance application of petroleum jelly in the private areas also works wonders. Keep a jar handy in your tack box.

Gloves

Gloves are mandatory only at FEI levels, but you'll see most riders wearing them in the lower-level tests because they create a look of elegance. Gloves also give you a better grip on the reins when your hands get sweaty, which is likely to happen at a show! White is the norm for competition. Buy a white pair or two and put them aside for show purposes. Choose any other color for schooling, but to achieve the best look and grip, buy gloves designed for riding, not work gloves or all-purpose cold weather gloves.

Caring for Your Tack and Riding Apparel

Because tack and riding apparel represent a significant financial investment, you'll want to take good care of them and preserve their longevity. Some people are tack-cleaning fanatics, and some aren't. I happen to fall into the latter category, but I do at least wipe off dust and sweat with warm water and a sponge or damp cloth after every ride. Every so often, you'll need to take your bridle apart and do a thorough cleaning. Remove the stirrup leathers and thoroughly clean the saddle, too. Always do this before a show to remove any telltale sign of dirt or dust. You want your tack to be sparkling clean and polished whenever you participate in a show or clinic. Cleaning equipment also gives you an opportunity to inspect closely for cracks, loose stitching, and other problems that could potentially break and compromise your safety.

After every ride, always rinse the bit to ensure that the surface is smooth and clean the next time you put it in your horse's mouth. This will help prevent your horse from feeling any discomfort from dry, hardened bits of grass, saliva, and other grime stuck to the surface and corners of the bit.

Synthetic tack is easy to wipe or hose off with warm water. Leather saddles and bridles can be cleaned with saddle soap. Take care not to get the leather too soapy, as this can have a drying effect. One trick to getting tack clean is to change your rinse water often, and rinse with a separate, clean sponge, so that you're not putting dirty water back on the piece you just cleaned.

Regular cleaning generally helps maintain the proper amount of moisture and suppleness in the leather, so you don't have to oil it that often. Overoiling leather can create more problems than it solves, causing stretching and molding, so use the oil sparingly. If you must oil, be sure to wipe off all excess oil, or it will rub off on your clothing next time you ride.

Polish metal hardware to a shine with a good metal polish, following the manufacturer's directions for use. Polishing looks super and helps slow the corrosion process. If you polish the bit's mouthpiece, be sure to rinse it thoroughly with hot water, or your horse may object to the taste.

Launder saddle pads in the washing machine after every use. Check the labels for washing instructions. Do not reuse a dirty saddle pad, as the dried sweat and dirt can rub and irritate the horse's back. Also, do not swap saddle pads from horse to horse, as this can spread skin diseases.

Launder or dry clean your show clothes after every use, per the manufacturer's instructions, and store them in garment bags. Wipe the dust from your show derby with a damp rag and store it in a hat box.

If you aren't sure how to care for or clean a particular piece of equipment, ask the tack store proprietor where you purchased the item. Tack shop owners are generally knowledgeable about the equipment and products they sell. Many are horsemen themselves and are usually well informed about the dress and tack requirements for various types of shows and classes. Because some tack shops cater to either western-riding or English-riding clientele, it's a good idea to ask around in the dressage community and find out where most of your fellow dressage riders shop.

Although ordering equipment online or through mail-order catalogs may be convenient, I have always found the personnel at the tack shops I frequent extremely helpful when I'm making my selections. In fact, I view them as a vital link in my ongoing education as a horse owner, because they often take time to offer advice, share their own experiences, and tell me about new products. When it comes to selecting, using, and caring for tack and riding apparel, these folks are your best resource.

Chapter Eight

Preparing for Your First Competition

To Show or Not to Show

To some, the challenges of competition are rewarding and exhilarating, while for others, the intense planning and preparation required just adds extra stress to their lives. Showing isn't for everyone, but if you've never done it, you and your horse should try out a local schooling show or two to see how you like it. You might get hooked, and you will certainly come away from the arena with your riding horizons expanded a bit. Above all, never allow competition and the desire to win to make you lose sight of the training process or interfere with your enjoyment of your horse.

Remember, dressage shows are different from most other horse shows, where several horses and riders compete in the ring at the same time. When executing a test at a dressage show, it's just you and your horse performing in front of the judge, with an audience of spectators looking on. Small details can make all the difference. Dressage is all about precision, and even having your horse on proper contact counts (see the three figures on the following page). Some riders find being in the spotlight in this way a bit unnerving, while others thrive on it.

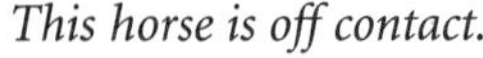

This horse is off contact.

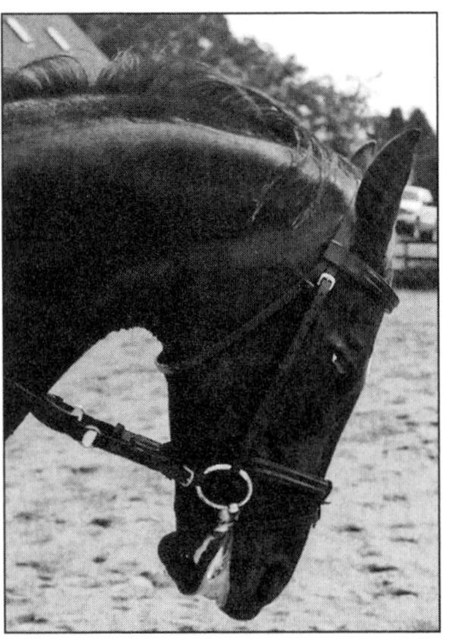

This horse is behind the vertical.

This horse is relaxed and on contact.

Riders compete in horse shows for many good reasons:

- To evaluate their training progress against others testing at the same level
- For the experience of handling their horse in new surroundings
- To win ribbons, money, prizes, and year-end awards through various equestrian organizations
- To promote their horse, farm, or training facility
- To learn by watching other riders compete
- To have fun and socialize with others who share a common interest

If your horse is a seasoned schoolmaster, he's been to lots of shows and likely will know what's expected of him when you turn down the centerline. Your first time in the ring will go much more smoothly if at least one of you has some experience!

However, if your horse has never been to a show, expect the worst and hope for the best. You can never predict how a horse is going to behave in strange, new surroundings. The exposure will be good training for him, but could prove to be a handful for you. If you aren't confident about handling him under such circumstances, have your instructor or another knowledgeable horse person with you to help.

Although you can start out on a small budget, showing horses can become an expensive hobby over time, considering the entry fees, travel costs, accommodations, and the investment in special tack, clothing, and equipment. You also need to consider the investment of time involved in lessons and training. Competition at Federation Equestre Internationale (FEI) levels is especially demanding and requires a full-time commitment.

At some point, you'll need to decide how involved in the hobby you can afford to get, in terms of both money and time, and arrange the necessary resources. But even if you decide that showing isn't your game, remember, you and your horse can still reap many benefits from dressage training without ever riding in front of a judge.

Choosing a Show

The type of show you choose to enter depends on where you and your horse are in your training. Green horses and green riders are better off starting small, at local nonrated shows, before progressing on to larger recognized shows. Your riding instructor can help you determine what type of show is most suitable for you to attend. Likewise, the tests you choose to ride at the show will depend on your current skills and abilities and on how comfortable you feel executing the test requirements.

Ride-a-Tests

While not a real show subject to the usual rules and regulations, ride-a-tests provide a good starting point for any horse and/or rider with little or no prior show experience. These loosely organized practice events are more casual and informal than schooling shows and are generally inexpensive to enter and attend. For these reasons, they offer an excellent opportunity for someone to experience riding a test in front of an audience for the first time, as well as for someone trying out a new test before moving on to an actual show. Similar in atmosphere to a riding clinic, the person judging usually takes time to give you some valuable pointers on improving your test score.

Ride-a-tests are typically arranged by a riding facility or club for the education of its clientele and interested participants from the surrounding community. Although ribbons may be given to the top-scoring rides, there are no points to count toward any formal awards, because it's not actual competition. Instead, ride-a-tests place more emphasis on learning, practice, and gaining experience in a quasi-competitive atmosphere.

Schooling Shows

If no ride-a-tests are available, another good way to start is to enter a schooling show in your area. The atmosphere at these smaller, unrecognized shows is typically casual and relaxed, giving nervous newcomers to the sport a chance to test their riding skills in public, in front of a judge, and still taste some showtime fun and excitement. More seasoned exhibitors often like to try out a new test at a schooling show first, to see how they'll score, before they perform the same test at a recognized show.

Because the focus is on schooling, the judges are generally more willing to share some pointers and constructive criticism. Schooling show organizers are generally more lenient about protocol and apparel, which makes this venue ideal for someone who hasn't delved into the hobby long enough to invest in expensive show equipment.

Recognized or Rated Shows

These shows are, of course, the real thing and represent a more serious and more expensive step up in your show endeavors. Typically organized by a local or state dressage club chapter, these shows are sanctioned by the horse show governing body (U.S. Equestrian Federation [USEF] and/or FEI) and offer riders an opportunity to compete for points and awards. Licensed judges score the tests, and these scores are used by the U.S. Dressage Foundation to calculate year-end awards.

Selecting Your Tests

If you're going to go to the expense, time, and trouble of entering and traveling to a show, especially a recognized show, you may as well make it worthwhile and ride at least two tests while you're there. That way, if either you or your horse is nervous enough to blow the first test, you have a chance to come back in the second and hopefully improve your score. According to the USEF *Rule Book*, horses are limited to a maximum of three rides per day at Fourth Level and below. Above Fourth Level, only two rides per day are permitted, because the tests are so demanding and difficult.

Your riding instructor will help you select tests that are appropriate to your skills and your horse's level of training. Typically, it is advisable to show at one level lower than what you're schooling at home. For example, if you're schooling at Training Level at home, consider selecting an Introductory Level test to ride at your first show. The more confident you feel about executing the gaits, figures, and movements, the better you'll perform, despite the jitters and all the other distractions that abound on show day.

Participation Requirements

Competitors are required to adhere to all current rules and regulations in and out of the ring, so you'd better read the USEF *Rule Book* and familiarize yourself with the dressage division section before you enter. You can view the *Rule Book* online at www.usef.org, or as a member request a printed copy or CD. International competitions are governed by FEI rules, which are covered in the FEI booklet *Rules for Dressage Events*.

Horses competing in USEF-recognized shows must have an identification number, which you include on the show entry form. For certain types of classes, your horse must also be properly recorded and registered with a breed organization.

Otherwise, both professional and amateur riders may compete on a horse of any breed, type, or sex. Ponies, however, cannot compete in certain types of classes, and these are clearly stated in the *Rule Book*.

A professional rider is someone who gets paid for riding, training, showing, and so forth. Professionals cannot show in classes designated for amateurs. The term *amateur* in this context does not mean "novice," but refers to someone who does not receive monetary reimbursement. Many amateurs are expert riders; they just don't get paid for it.

Some age restrictions apply to participation in dressage competition:

- The horse must be at least 36 months of age to compete under saddle. (Younger horses may be shown in-hand.)
- Horses competing above Fourth Level must be at least 6 years old.
- Horses competing at Grand Prix Level have to be at least 7 years old.

As with racing horses, a dressage horse's age is counted from January 1 of its birth year to January 1 of the current competition year. These rules help ensure that the horse's training is not rushed and that he is not pushed into performing advanced movements before he has attained sufficient growth and physical development.

Age requirements also govern a rider's participation in the dressage division as follows:

- Riders may compete as Juniors from the beginning of the year in which they turn 14 until the end of the year in which they turn 18.
- Similarly, the Young Riders age group runs from 16 to 21.
- Riders compete as Adults from the beginning of the year in which they turn 22.

Entering a Show

Dressage club chapters generally provide their members with an annual Omnibus that includes dates and details for the recognized shows scheduled within the club's region. When you and your instructor decide what show you should enter, contact the show secretary and request the necessary forms. You'll receive a Prize List, which lists the classes offered in the competition and the judges who will be officiating. This document also covers pertinent details such as stabling, accommodations, and fees.

The Entry Form is what you need to complete and return to the show secretary, with the appropriate entry fee, before the closing date. This ensures that you will have a ride time scheduled. Make sure you complete all information requested on the form. The show organization requires the information to record and track competitors' accomplishments. If you have difficulty filling out the entry form, or if you don't understand something that is requested, call the show secretary well in advance and ask for help.

The Negative Coggins Test

Proof of a negative Coggins test (a blood test that determines whether a horse has equine infectious anemia) is generally required for admission to almost any show in the United States. If you don't already have a current Coggins certificate that you can photocopy and mail with your entry, you need to arrange for your veterinarian to perform this test several weeks in advance of the show date.

The blood test goes to an authorized lab for processing, and then the results are mailed to you. Be sure to allow adequate time to receive the certificate in the mail. Most people who show regularly schedule a Coggins test with their routine annual vaccinations, as the results remain current for only one year.

Entries submitted after the closing date are accepted as post entries at the discretion of the show management, depending on space availability. If an opening date is given for the show, your entry form cannot be postmarked any earlier than this date.

It's important to honor the closing date protocol, because the show secretary must schedule the ride times for dressage tests in advance and contact the riders by phone or mail to let them know what time they are expected to ride. That's why you can't just show up on the day of the competition and sign in, as is often the case with some other types of horse shows. The exception to this is when a competitor scratches from the show, leaving a vacant time slot to fill.

Who Does What at a Show

A lot of work goes into planning and organizing a horse show, and most of it is accomplished by volunteers. The local dressage chapters exist primarily to organize shows and promote their sport, so that more people can experience the beauty and traditions of classical riding. As a dressage rider, it is well worth your time to join and support the events your local club puts on. A list of these organizations is included in the back of this book.

Volunteers

One of the best ways to learn about dressage shows is to volunteer to work at one, before you ever get involved in actually competing. Although judges are normally paid for their time, most shows rely on volunteers to perform other essential functions, from posting scores to serving food, particularly at the local and regional levels. Often, to make sure that they have enough human resources to put on shows, many dressage clubs require their members to put in a certain number of volunteer hours each year. One of the toughest jobs is the volunteer coordinator, who recruits volunteers, assigns the jobs, and helps pull the entire volunteer workforce together.

Scribes

Perhaps the most educational job, and one of the best ways to learn dressage from the judge's point of view, is to work as a scribe at a show. A scribe sits next to the judge and writes down the judge's comments and scores for each test. This frees the judge to concentrate solely on the competitor. The judge dictates his thoughts throughout the test, and because of this running commentary, a scribe gains valuable insight into what the judge is looking for in each movement. To be a scribe, you need to be able to write quickly and have good penmanship. Some knowledge of the tests to be scored is also helpful. As a first-time scribe, you will be assigned with a judge who is scoring lower-level tests.

Runners and Scorers

Runners volunteer to collect the completed test scores from the scribes and carry them to the scorers. Scorers add up the rider's test points and calculate the percentage score for the ride. These volunteers are usually cloistered away in a back room of the show office, pecking away furiously at their calculators, and they don't get to see much of the action at the show. However, if the weather is really lousy outside, being indoors all day is not such a bad place to be.

Gatekeepers

If you volunteer to work as a gatekeeper, you'll get to watch other riders perform their tests, but you'll have to be outside in the elements all day, unless you're lucky enough to get assigned to an indoor arena. The function of the gatekeeper is to open and shut the gate each time a competitor enters and leaves the arena. Also, after a certain number of rides, the gatekeeper rolls the centerline with a roller to flatten out the churned up footing. This helps keep the centerline visible for the competitors and judges.

Ring Stewards and Show Managers

The ring stewards volunteer to inspect the bits and saddlery and keep riders apprised of how many riders are ahead of them and who's on deck to ride his test next. The show manager oversees the entire event organization from start to finish and is responsible for hiring the judges and other paid personnel.

Technical Delegates

Technical delegates (TDs) are not volunteers, but are official USEF representatives who make sure that the rules are followed. They are trained and licensed as either uppercase *R* for *registered* TDs or lowercase *r* for *recorded* technical delegates. For all matters relating to rules, or to ask permission to speak to a judge, the TD is the person to contact. Speaking directly to a judge without permission is prohibited.

Judges

The judges officiating at a show are sometimes referred to as the ground jury. They are paid for their expertise, and it's important to understand that judges do not arbitrarily compare one horse to another, but hold each horse and rider and their performance to an accepted standard.

If there is only one judge, he sits outside the arena at the letter C. If two judges are used, one sits at C, and the other is placed at either B or E. When there are three judges, one is placed at C, the second is at B or E, and the third is at H or M. The *Rule Book* specifies precise measurements for positioning the judges relative to these letters. The enclosure provided for each judge may be a booth, tent, car, or trailer.

Judges must complete extensive training and pass an examination before they can become licensed at a certain level. They are also required to attend refresher courses periodically to maintain their licensed status.

On Prize Lists, you'll usually see a letter listed beside each judge's name. The letter assigned to a judge indicates the training that judge has received and what levels he is qualified to judge:

- *L* = a *learner* judge. This is a beginner judge who has completed the initial phase of a judge's training. You'll encounter these judges officiating at schooling shows.
- Lowercase *r* = a *recorded* judge who is licensed to officiate through Second Level.
- Uppercase *R* = a *registered* judge who can officiate through Fourth Level.
- *S* = a *senior* judge who can officiate through the FEI levels at competitions held within the United States.
- *I* = an *international* judge who can officiate at international FEI competitions.
- *C* = an FEI *candidate* who is learning to be an international judge.
- *O* = an FEI *official* who is trained and qualified to judge all the way up to the highest level of competition, the Olympics.

Grooming Your Horse for a Show

Your horse and tack must be sparkling clean for a show. You'll need to begin some preparations in advance, such as pulling the horse's mane so that you can braid it more easily. The day before the show, have your horse bathed (weather permitting), clipped, and braided, and everything packed and ready. That way, you'll only have to worry about touch-ups the day of the show, and you won't feel rushed.

Grooming for a show starts like any other normal grooming session, except you spend more time on the details. First, pick out the hooves with a hoof pick, as you would before and after each ride. As always, use the opportunity to inspect the feet for cracks or other problems and the shoes for signs of looseness. If you notice anything amiss in the days before the show, get your farrier to check it out right away.

Curry the coat briskly, moving the curry comb with the lay of the hair in a somewhat circular fashion. This helps loosen the dead hair and deep-down dirt and bring it to the surface. Whisk the dirt away with a stiff-bristle body brush, always brushing with the hair, never against it. Use a soft-bristle brush on sensitive areas, such as the face, legs, and belly. Follow up with an overall toweling to remove any fine dirt the brush missed.

Clipping

Before bathing your horse, show clip him to give him a neater look. Then you can rinse away the loose hairs during his bath. If you've never clipped a horse before, or if you aren't sure how well your horse tolerates electric clippers, ask a more experienced horse person to assist you the first time and show you what to do. If the horse strongly objects to clippers, you can use scissors, but the job will take a lot longer.

Show clipping involves shaving the whiskers off the muzzle, trimming the shaggy hair off the fetlock area, and trimming a bridle path behind the ears where the bridle's crown piece rests. Also tidy up around the outside edges of the ears, but leave the hair inside the ears undisturbed, as it helps keep out flies and dirt.

Some people body clip their horses, but this is recommended only when the horse stays indoors a lot and is routinely blanketed or otherwise protected from biting insects and fluctuating temperatures. But if your horse will return to life out in the pasture after his show, he'll need his hair to shield his skin from the elements, regardless of the season.

Giving Your Horse a Bath

If your horse is really dirty or muddy, he'll need a bath, climate permitting. If it's too cold where you live, simply put some extra elbow grease behind the brush and curry comb and wipe the coat clean with warm, moist towels.

Tack shops sell shampoos and conditioners for horses and can recommend good products. Choose products labeled for use on equines, and avoid detergents, as these can be harsh enough to deplete the skin of natural oils and rob the coat of its shine. If your horse has stained white markings, there are also specialty products for getting those socks and stockings clean. Whatever products you select, read the label and follow the directions for use.

Some stables have wash stalls with hot and cold running water, but if yours doesn't, fill two buckets: one with warm clear water for wetting and rinsing and the other for mixing the shampoo. Wet the horse's coat down first using a sponge or water hose. Take care not to let the horse stand in drafts or get chilled, especially if you have access only to cold water from a hose or pump. Sponge the sudsy shampoo mixture over the horse's entire body and work it in with a mitt or your hands. Avoid getting shampoo in or near the eyes. Because most horses dislike being sprayed around the head, clean the face with a wet sponge or towel and rinse the same way.

When you have rinsed thoroughly and removed all traces of suds, use a sweat scraper over the horse to remove excess water from the coat. This helps the hair dry out faster. Towel dry the legs and face and rub down the rest of the body to absorb as much remaining dampness as possible.

Pulling and Braiding Manes

Dressage horses are traditionally shown with braided manes, although this is not a requirement. The purpose of braiding is to lift the hair off the neck so the judge can see the horse's carriage and topline. French or hunter braids are most common, although other styles are sometimes seen, largely depending on the breed of the horse.

A mane is easier to braid if it is kept short, about three or four inches long, and even. To do this, many dressage riders pull the longer mane hairs, a few at a time, throughout the year to maintain the desired shape, thickness, and length for show season. This is rather easily accomplished by spending ten or fifteen minutes of your daily routine on the task over a period of several months. It doesn't hurt the horse, as long as you pull only a few hairs each time. But if you procrastinate, you can't pull the whole overgrown mane the day before the show. It simply takes too long and would cause the horse discomfort by doing too much at once. That being the case, your other option, in a pinch, is to trim the mane with scissors. This may not look as natural as a mane that has been thinned and tapered by pulling, but it will make do for braiding purposes.

To pull a mane, you first comb a small section of hair free of tangles and snarls. Then hold the longest portion of the mane in one hand and backcomb toward the roots with several swift, upward strokes, as if teasing the hair. This pushes most of the hair back toward the neck's crest, except for the longer strands you are holding. Wrap just a few (five or so) of these longer strands around the comb and give a yank, pulling the hairs out.

The idea is to separate the longer hairs all along the mane in this manner and pull them out, just a few strands at a time. Most horses don't seem to flinch at a few hairs being pulled, but never attempt to yank out a huge chunk of hair at once. Doing so will hurt the horse, and he may express his discomfort in ways you won't appreciate. Also, if the horse begins to get restless during the procedure, he may be getting annoyed or uncomfortable with the pulling. Stop and come back to it another day.

As you work on one section of mane at a time, a few minutes each day, you will eventually thin and shorten the mane. By now, it should be obvious why this method is so time-consuming and must be begun months ahead of the show.

Although fairly simple and straightforward, braiding requires some practice to get the braids neat and even. It's a good thing to practice on rainy days when you can't ride. I'll explain the basics here, but most people adapt their own preferred braiding technique after several trial runs.

For your braiding kit you'll need:

- An apron with pockets or a tool kit to tie around your waist
- A spray bottle filled with water
- A mane comb
- Hair clips
- Rubber bands or thread that matches the color of the mane
- White yarn or tape (optional)
- A latch hook tool
- Scissors
- Hair spray or styling gel

Stand on a step stool or mounting block and comb the entire length of mane to smooth it out. Then go back and separate the hair into sections, about one and a half inches wide. Use the hair clips to hold the hair out of your way as you work. Starting at the head, separate one section into three strands and tightly braid the strands together, one over the other. The hair is easier to handle if you dampen it first with water from your spray bottle. If you're using yarn, braid about a four-inch piece in with the hair, starting about halfway down. Secure the braid at the end with a rubber band, or tie it off with the yarn or thread. Use hair spray or gel on each braid for extra hold.

In this way, work down the neck toward the withers until you have a row of evenly spaced braids, as shown in the figure on this page. Then go back and pull the end of each braid up through the top of the braid, using the latch hook tool to grab the end and draw it through. Secure this knot with the yarn or another rubber band, and clip off any excess yarn or thread. Don't forget to braid the forelock as well.

If your test is scheduled in the morning hours of the show, you'll need to braid the night before. If you ride later in the afternoon, you can braid the morning of the show, if you think you'll have adequate time to do so.

Horses are notorious about rubbing out braids against fence posts and stall walls, so be sure to take your kit with you to fix any that may come loose. You can also buy a hood that slips over the neck and helps protect the braids.

Braiding a mane that looks this nice takes some practice to get good at it.

Tails

If your horse has accumulated burrs or tangles in his tail, work them out with your fingers and then gently comb out the tail, taking care not to pull out too many long hairs. You'll need to trim the top of the tail around the dock to make the shorter hairs that stick out in all directions in that area blend in more and lie flat with the longer hairs. Also trim in on the sides of the dock just a little for shape and contour, giving the tail a neat, smooth look. You can accomplish this with either scissors or electric trimmers. But be careful not to overdo it; you don't want your horse to have a naked-looking rear end. Rather, the purpose of trimming the tail is to allow the judge a better view of how well the horse uses his hindquarters as he goes through his paces.

After you finish trimming the tail, dip it in a bucket of warm water and wash it with horse shampoo. Certain equine shampoos are formulated especially for mane and tail hair to condition and minimize tangling. Take great care to rinse the hair thoroughly, as any residue left in could cause the horse to itch and rub his tail, creating a scraggly, mangled mess of your handiwork.

Dressage horses are typically shown with their tails banged, or cut straight across the bottom, instead of tapered at the end. When the tail is dry, hold the tail straight down and evenly in one hand. Use scissors to snip off just a little of the length at a time. Let the tail go and step back to gauge the straightness of your handiwork. Continue trimming as needed to achieve as straight and even a cut as possible. Ideally, a banged tail hangs about fetlock length or slightly higher.

After preparing the tail for a show, some people like to braid it loosely, fold it up, and put it in a knee sock or tail bag to keep it clean and protected. Then simply unbraid it and brush it out before your test.

Cleaning Tack

If you can afford it, keep separate sets of tack for showing and schooling, which can make your show preparation a lot easier.

After every show, simply clean the tack thoroughly and store it in a dry place. Next time you get it out, spot check it and spruce up any areas that may have gotten dull or dusty during storage.

Always wipe your tack clean with a damp cloth after each use to remove sweat and dust, and periodically take everything apart for a deep, thorough cleaning. Rinse the bit with clean water after every ride. This prevents dried saliva and gunk from caking in the corners and causing mouth soreness.

How you clean your tack and what products you use depends on whether the gear is made of leather or a synthetic material. These days, some of the synthetics look like leather and clean up nicely with water and elbow grease. Real leather requires a special leather cleaner and conditioner to prevent drying and cracking. The tack shop where you purchase your gear can recommend appropriate products.

To clean a bridle, take it apart and clean each piece. It takes some practice to put the parts back together properly, but if you clean your tack as often as you should, this will soon become second nature. Use a sponge or an old, soft-bristle toothbrush to scrub away stubborn accumulations of grime, especially around the buckles and keepers.

Remove the stirrup leathers from the saddle, and remove the stirrup pads from the irons. Clean all parts separately and let dry before reassembling. Avoid oiling leather just before a show, as the excess will wear off on your white riding breeches. These stains are hard to wash out of the pants later. Better to oil leather after a show, if needed, and before storing the tack away.

Packing for a Show

Anything can happen at a show, so you can never be too prepared. The basic items you'll need to pack for yourself include:

- All riding apparel required for your test level, including jacket, breeches or jodhpurs, and tall riding boots or jodhpur boots
- Boot pulls and boot jack

- Boot polish and cleaner
- White shirt and sport socks (pack extra clean ones)
- Undergarments that won't show under white or light-colored pants
- Tie, choker, or stock tie with stock pin
- Hunt cap, derby, or top hat, as required
- Safety helmet
- Riding whip (make sure it's regulation length)
- Gloves
- Belt
- Inclement weather gear
- Blunt metal spurs, as required
- Hairnet, hair clips, hair spray, and related accessories
- Smock or apron for keeping your show clothes clean
- Desitin or Vaseline for chafing problems and saddle sores
- Toiletries, cosmetics, and mirror
- Sleepover items, if staying overnight
- Street clothes
- A folding chair
- Personal items, such as medications, eyeglasses, and contacts, as needed
- Basic first aid supplies such as Band-Aid bandages, antibacterial spray or ointment, and aspirin or ibuprofen
- Spot cleaning supplies for touching up soiled riding clothes (keep a blow dryer handy at the show for drying damp touch-ups)
- A travel sewing kit for fixing tears or replacing buttons

- Checkbook, cash, or credit card
- Cooler with snacks and drinks
- All required paperwork and identification, including current Coggins test certificate, membership cards, driver's license, and your horse's registration papers, as applicable

Your horse requires even more gear. The Prize List will note what type of stabling is available on the show grounds and whether sawdust or shavings will be provided for stalls. At one-day local shows, stabling is often unavailable, and riders must show from their trailers. If this is the case for your first show, make sure your horse is trained to stand quietly tied to the trailer.

Here's a basic checklist that will most certainly expand over time as you travel more and more with your horse:

- Saddle, bridle, girth, and stirrups
- Tack trunk or portable saddle rack
- Extra stirrup leathers (in case of breakage)
- Extra girth (in case of breakage)
- Saddle pads (bring extras)
- Extra pair of reins (in case one breaks)
- Halter and lead ropes (pack extras, in case of breakage, and always use a leather or breakaway halter for trailering)
- Grooming supplies: brushes, curry comb, mane comb, plenty of towels, hoof pick, and hoof dressing or polish
- Bathing supplies: sweat scraper, horse shampoo, and sponges
- Braiding kit
- Fly spray

- Shipping boots and head bumper for protection during the trailer ride
- Other protective boots and wraps, as needed
- First aid kit for horses, including electrolytes (ask your vet)
- Salt block
- Hay and feed, as needed
- Hay net
- Water (if not available at the show grounds, or if your horse won't drink strange-tasting water)
- Feed and water buckets
- Wash buckets
- Horse treats
- Blankets, coolers, and fly sheets, as needed
- Liniment
- Stall/trailer bedding, as needed
- Stall/trailer cleaning supplies: muck bucket, wheelbarrow, and muck rake or shovel
- Lunge line and lunge whip
- Tack cleaning supplies

The Night Before

Your horse is groomed. Your tack is clean. Your show clothes are packed. Pack your trailer the evening before the show, if possible. Run down your checklist again to make sure you haven't forgotten something. Getting everything prepared ahead of time will help you relax your mind and body.

A Word about Dogs

Plan to leave your dog at home. Some shows prohibit dogs on the grounds, so if you must bring man's best friend, make sure this is permissible, and keep him on a leash and under your control at all times. While your horse may be well accustomed to dogs, others may not be. Plus, some horses are hyper at shows and more easily excitable by the strange sights and sounds.

Even if your dog is quiet and well behaved, he could innocently and inadvertently spook someone's horse with potentially disastrous results. You could even be held liable for injuries, so consider the risks carefully before deciding to bring your dog. This advice also applies if you're attending a show solely as a spectator.

Now is the time to prepare yourself mentally by taking some down time to rest. Do whatever you need to do to ensure that you get a good night's sleep the night before the show. If exercise helps you relax and recharge, do it. Yoga and meditation are particularly helpful for calming and centering the inner self. If a glass of wine works better for your show nerves, so be it. Just don't overdo the alcohol. If you're hungover or dehydrated the next day, it could negatively affect your performance.

Set aside some time to review in your mind and on paper the tests you are going to ride. To check your memorization of the test, give a copy to a family member and call out the movements. Just before bedtime, picture yourself in the show arena, having the best ride of your life. Visualize each movement at its best in your mind. Feel your confidence and the energy and impulsion that emanates from your horse. Imagine yourself winning and taking home a blue ribbon or trophy. Take this image to bed with you and let your subconscious absorb it during the night.

Sleep well and awake refreshed. Eat a good breakfast. The day ahead is going to be busy!

Chapter Nine

Riding a Dressage Test

Preparing for the Test at Home

You've submitted your entry forms and committed yourself to participating in a dressage show, perhaps your first one. You and your instructor have also decided what test(s) you are going to ride at the show. That accomplished, your next step is to obtain a current copy of the test(s) you plan to ride and start practicing the figures and movements at home. Concentrate on quality and correctness. Do not drill the horse over and over the same patterns in the order required on the test, or he may begin to anticipate and execute transitions before you ask him. If the horse appears to be anticipating during a test, this could possibly affect your scores in a negative way.

Dressage is, after all, precision riding, and the horse isn't supposed to do anything until you ask him. If the test calls for a movement or transition at letter C, it must happen on the letter, not before, not after. Much easier said than done. This measures the rider's skill at preparing the horse adequately for the required exercise, as well as the horse's obedience and submission. Submission in the context of dressage carries no negative connotations, but instead refers to the horse's willingness to please and perform and to his apparent harmony with his rider.

Remember that dressage tests are designed to give the judge seated behind the letter C the best view of certain movements, especially those executed down the center line and quarter lines of the arena. From this viewpoint, the judge can see very well whether your horse is weaving to one side or the other on the center line, and whether he is tracking straight. So when practicing at home, don't neglect your entry at A up to the halt and salute, or the strike-off into the gait that follows.

Achieving straightness on the center line is not as easy as it looks and reveals how well balanced and effective the rider's aids are on both sides of the horse. As you practice exercises down the center line, visualize your legs and reins creating a channel that your horse shoots straight through, so narrow that he can neither waver one step right nor left. In addition, keep your eyes focused on a point straight ahead and aim for it. If the horse steps, say, to the left of the line, you need more leg aid pressure on that side to hold him straight. At the same time, check whether you're applying too much pressure from the right leg, thus pushing him to the left. If he goes straight, you're doing it right.

The best way to practice a dressage test is to break the whole down into smaller sections and work on pieces of it at a time, but not always in the same order. Finally, put it all together at the end of some of your schooling sessions, to test how well you've memorized the sequence.

Memorizing the Test

Always memorize your test, just like you would memorize a speech or a poem, regardless of whether you plan to use a reader at the show. Even when someone reads the test aloud for you, you still need to know what's coming up next so you can prepare in advance. Remember, staying one step ahead of your horse is all part of being a thinking rider.

One helpful way to learn a test is to draw it out on paper. Sketch several rectangles for the arena and notate the letters around the sides. Then draw the patterns, figures, and movements in the same sequence that you would ride them. Label the rectangles so you can refer to them later during practice. This method also helps you memorize where the letters are located around the arena, which you need to know if you're going to continue participating in the sport.

Visualization

Another helpful technique for learning a test is to visualize riding it in your head, or your *mind's eye.* Sit quietly in a comfortable place, close your eyes, and breathe in and out deeply for several minutes. When you are relaxed, mentally picture yourself riding the test with confidence and correctness. Try to see and feel the action as if you were actually astride your horse. Visualize where you are at each step in the arena. See and feel yourself pass each letter and move on to the next required movement. The mind is a powerful tool, and with vivid visualization techniques you can program your subconscious with a correct mental image so that the brain can more readily tell the muscles in your body what to do.

To program a correct image, however, you must know what the correct movement looks and feels like to visualize it accurately. This is why you must observe more advanced riders and work with an instructor to achieve your goals. For example, if you're trying to learn to ride a correct shoulder-in, watch others do it to see what the movement is supposed to look like. An instructor can demonstrate the exercise for you, explain the proper aids, and then watch you apply them, correcting as needed. But it will be hard for you to visualize the movement correctly until you can also *feel* it correctly. Once you've executed the movement at least once correctly in real life, get to work on your visualization technique right away.

I use visualization quite often and find it extremely helpful, even for adjusting small but important position problems that seem too stubborn to go away on their own. For example, when I was first learning how to ride, my toes pointed out to the side, and my legs invariably crept too far forward. While mounted, I could point my toes forward and push my legs back under me, but they wouldn't stay put for long. No matter how hard I tried, I seemed to constantly fight against my leg position.

Such common faults generally result from the rider clutching and holding on with the lower leg or thighs, instead of maintaining balance properly, from a correct seat and body position. To fix these bad habits and others, my instructor put me on the longe line and helped me work up to riding without stirrups and reins. This ultimately helped me gain confidence and develop a more independent seat, which is essential before you can move on to the more complex dressage maneuvers.

To complement my training, I observed good riders in the saddle, both in person and on videos. Then I visualized myself riding that way, imagining myself as relaxed and poised as they looked, and zooming in on the lower leg for a good mental picture of the toes pointed forward, the heels down, and the leg properly aligned with the rest of the body. I focused on other problem parts, too, such as my shoulders that needed to be squared back, because the problem was really my whole position, not just the legs. Sometimes, when you focus too intently on correcting just one part of your position, something else goes awry. So you also need to zoom out and picture the correct whole, to keep things in perspective. Eventually, with good instruction and practice, my body learned to relax and do things right (at least more often than not), but I'm convinced that visualization helped it all happen faster.

Riding the Halt

The halt in a dressage test is much more than just stopping the horse and, as with everything else related to this sport, it's not as easy as it looks. In a test, the first halt is at X, which marks the middle of the dressage arena. There's no letter X placed in the center, so you use your peripheral vision to sight the spot on the center line between letters E and B. The ideal halt must be straight and square, and it must happen on the letter X, not two steps before or after.

To achieve a square halt, the horse has to be on the bit and engaged from behind. A halt doesn't start with the rider pulling back on the reins to stop the horse, as many people believe. If you use the crude method of just hauling back on the reins, the horse throws his head up and hollows his back. He'll stop, but you've lost your contact, roundness, and engagement. This is not what you want to happen, because your horse is no longer together. You want the hindquarters to come up under the horse and his face to remain on the vertical, or slightly in front of the vertical.

The halt is actually a forward transition that begins with the rider sitting more deeply and heavily in the saddle and tightening her seat to drive (not shove) the horse's hindquarters forward into her hands. The rider then resists any further forward motion by setting the hands (or stopping the hands from following the horse's head motion). In other words, you push the horse forward into the bit, but at the same time, you quietly restrain with your hands. When the horse comes up against this restraint, he stops.

By executing a halt the proper way, instead of just hauling back on the reins, the hindquarters come up under the horse. His rear end is not strung out behind him (as it is in the figure on this page), and his back remains rounded, not hollow. The horse remains engaged and on the bit, and he will be easier to move off the spot at

A strung-out halt with hind leg too far back.

This rider has thrown away her contact at the free walk, which would cost her points in a test. Note her hollow back and extended arms; she should sit back, with shoulders square, and feed out the reins slowly.

X in this manner into any gait you ask of him. Never sacrifice correctness, not even at a free walk (as happened in the figure on this page).

On a well-trained horse that is sensitive to the lightest of aids, you should be able to stop the horse solely with your seat, without reins. This is a good exercise to practice when riding a schoolmaster during a longe line session. Drop the reins and try to stop the horse simply by sitting back more heavily and more deeply in the saddle.

The Salute

Along with the halt, dressage tests begin and end with the traditional salute to the judge who sits at C. Although the first halt and salute take place at X, the final halt and salute may occur at G or I, depending on the test and level. G and I are located on the center line closer to the judge at C. Also, riders performing freestyles (dressage set to music) may choose where they want to halt and salute.

To salute, the rider first takes the reins in one hand. Failure to take the reins into one hand constitutes an error of the test and incurs penalty points. The rules don't specifically state which hand to use, but it's customary to place the reins in the left hand and use the right to salute. Whichever hand you intend to salute with, make sure the whip (if one is allowed) is in your other hand before you enter at A. Otherwise, you'll have to switch it gracefully before you salute.

Women drop the right arm to their side and briefly nod the head in a polite bow to the judge, as shown in the figure on this page. Men do the same, except they also remove their hat (unless it's a safety helmet with a chin harness) with the same hand that they are going to lower for the salute. The judge acknowledges the salute with a nod or by sitting down if she is standing as the rider enters. This simple action grants the rider permission to proceed with the test or, if the test is over, to leave the arena.

During a dressage test, the rider executes a square halt at X and salutes the judge. This is what it looks like from the judge's viewpoint.

Understanding a Dressage Test

In printed format, dressage tests are often laid out on an 8.5-by-14-inch sheet of paper, folded in half. The front cover identifies the test and describes its purpose for assessing a particular stage of training. There may also be instructions or comments that explain how the test should be ridden, for example, whether trot work is to be ridden rising (posting) or sitting.

The actual test is arranged in columns. The first column lists the letter or letters where each movement or transition is to be executed. The second column, titled Test, describes the movements required. The next column lists the Directive Ideas, which explain what the judge is looking for in each movement. For example, straightness on center line is a common directive listed for the rider's entry at A. As you practice each phase of the test, review the corresponding directives to help you understand what quality is being stressed for each movement. The directives represent important stages of training, so if you are unclear as to what they mean, ask your instructor. You are less likely to score well on any test until you have a clear understanding of why you're doing what you're doing at each stage of training.

The blank columns to the right of the Directive Ideas are for recording and totaling the points, and the last column allows the judge (or scribe) to write in remarks or comments beside each movement. The wise rider understands that scoring is subjective and pays greater attention to the judge's comments, which can provide an opportunity to learn and improve scores the next time.

At the bottom of the page are the Collective Marks, which the judge adds when your test is complete. These assess the horse's gaits, impulsion, and submission, as well as the rider's position, seat, and effectiveness of aids. These marks carry a fixed coefficient, which is a multiplier for that particular item. For example, if the judge gives you a 6 for impulsion, and the coefficient is 2, then your total score for that item is 12. Coefficients indicate the degree of emphasis being placed on particular requirements within a given test.

How a Dressage Test Is Scored

The Collective Marks and each movement within the test receive a score on a scale from 0 to 10, with 10 being the highest. The U.S. Equestrian Foundation (USEF) *Rule Book* clearly explains the scale of marks. Here's what they mean:

10 Excellent
9 Very good
8 Good
7 Fairly good
6 Satisfactory
5 Sufficient
4 Insufficient
3 Fairly bad
2 Bad
1 Very bad
0 Not executed

A 0 means you did practically nothing of that required movement. For example, if your horse is supposed to execute a working canter from E to H, but instead just trots faster, you'll get a 0. Typical scores hover midway, around 5 and 6. Marks of 7 or 8 mean you did really well on that particular figure or movement. Higher marks are handed out less commonly, generally reserved for a truly spectacular execution of a particular movement.

If you commit an error during the test, it will cost you penalty points that are subtracted from the score total. An error constitutes going off course, missing a movement, taking a wrong turn, rising at the trot when sitting is required, or doing something else that isn't on the test. Because most errors are caused by show nerves or by not knowing the test very well, they often can be avoided with better preparation.

Depending on the nature of the infraction, the judge may count off the points without interrupting the test or sound a warning whistle or bell. In the case of the latter, you should halt and heed the judge's instructions before continuing. It's okay to ride closer to the judge to hear what she has to say, if necessary.

Each test has a maximum number of possible points that can be received. This is printed somewhere on the test sheet, usually on the front. The scorer totals all the marks received, including the collective marks, and divides that total by the maximum number of possible points. This gives you a percentage score, the higher the better.

As soon as the scorers can complete their calculations, scores are posted on a bulletin board, usually in the vicinity of the show office, or other public viewing area on the grounds. The rider with the highest total score wins. The rider with the next highest score places second, and so forth. In the case of a tie, the rider with the highest collective marks wins. If the collective marks are tied, then the judge has to decide the winner or let the tie stand.

Elimination

Some infractions can result in elimination from a class or the entire competition, depending on their nature. One of the most common causes of elimination, late entry into the arena, is also one of the easiest to prevent. Simply pay attention to the time. Also, before the start of each test the judge rings a warning bell. If it's your time to ride, you have forty-five seconds after the bell rings to enter the arena. Exceeding forty-five seconds is cause for elimination.

Some other causes for elimination include:

- A professional riding in a class for amateurs (this is called misrepresentation or inappropriate entry)
- All four of the horse's feet leaving the arena, with or without the rider (a fall in and of itself is not cause for elimination but penalizes the movement and the collective marks)

- Any resistance or refusal lasting longer than twenty seconds when the horse is being asked to perform a particular movement
- Blood on the horse (except from insect bites)
- Cruelty to the horse, which includes excessive use of whip and spurs, among other things listed in the *Rule Book*
- Direct rule violations
- Dress code violations (elimination is at the judge's discretion)
- Failure to wear the competitor number
- Marked lameness
- Three errors of the course (e.g., going off course, taking a wrong turn, and omitting a movement)
- Tying down a horse's tongue
- Unauthorized assistance from the sidelines (e.g., if someone is reading your test aloud for you, that person can only read the test, and not say anything else that might be construed as coaching)
- Use of illegal drugs
- Use of illegal equipment (e.g., martingales, seat covers, boots, and leg bandages are prohibited in the competition arena, along with illegal bits and other items listed in the *Rule Book*)

The USEF *Rule Book* explains these and other causes for penalty or elimination. As a competitor, you should be familiar with them and keep abreast of any rule changes that are enacted from year to year. Ignorance is never an excuse, so let the *Rule Book* be your show bible.

Scratches

When a competitor withdraws herself from a class or competition, it's called a scratch. You may be forced to scratch, for example, if your horse suddenly turns ill or lame or throws a shoe and there's no farrier to put it back on. Contact the show management as soon as you know you need to scratch. The rules require certain paperwork for scratches, so you can't just fail to show up and not say anything to anyone. Also, be aware that entry fees generally aren't refunded in the event of a scratch on the day of the show or after the show's closing date.

If a rider ahead of you scratches, you may be given an opportunity to move up your time and ride sooner, which you may or may not choose to do.

Warming up at a Show

At a show, competitors are permitted to warm up their horses only in designated areas, and they usually receive a map of the grounds indicating where these areas are. Show management may also ask competitors to adhere to certain guidelines when longeing horses. At all times, courtesy and safety should prevail.

The purpose of a warm-up is to get the horse relaxed in his surroundings and focused on the upcoming task, as shown in the figure on the next page. And, as with any other athlete, the warm-up period stretches, flexes, and prepares the muscles for the upcoming physical demands that will be placed on them.

Having worked with your horse at home, you should know how long and how intense of a warm-up he needs. However, in new surroundings he may have a bit more of an edge that needs trimming with a longer warm-up, but don't try to wear him out. You don't want him to look tired and dragging during the test. A little of that edge can actually work to your advantage in the competition arena, as long as it's controlled, giving your horse a more energetic presence.

To help your horse relax, try to ride him the same way you would ride him at home. If the two of you have established a trusting

Warming up on the longe helps take that nervous edge off a fresh horse before you ride.

relationship, a familiar routine will help reassure him that you're still in control and, therefore, everything is going to be okay.

Warm-up under saddle can be a scary experience for someone new to showing, because you are in the warm-up arena with so many other riders, and everyone seems to be moving in a different direction. Also, some horses may be excitable or even unruly in their new surroundings. The pace for the day is already hectic, so you need to have your show nerves in control here. This is also where it is definitely more comforting to be on a seasoned schoolmaster, who's used to being ridden among other horses at shows, instead of a greenie who's so scared he's ready to explode.

To an onlooker, the warm-up area may look like mass chaos with riders going in all directions, but there are some basic guidelines that help maintain order:

- Ride in the same direction as the majority of the other riders, and when they reverse, you reverse.
- It is customary to pass riders going in the opposite direction with your left to their left.

- If the situation warrants that you pass right to right, it is courteous to call out as you approach, "Passing on your right," or some similar verbal indication, so that the other rider will know what you're going to do.
- Pass riders moving in the same direction on the inside, taking care not to get too close.
- Give other horses plenty of clearance; circle out of their way if you need to, and *never* ride up close on the back-end of one.
- To practice halts, pirouettes, and similar slow movements, move off the rail toward the middle of the warm-up area.
- Yield to riders who are practicing lateral movements or extended gaits.
- If a horse goes ballistic or dumps his rider, stop what you're doing until the situation gets under control.

For warm-ups, the same rules regarding saddlery and equipment apply. With just a few exceptions, you can't use anything in the warm-up or other training areas that's not permitted in the competition arena. You can, however, put protective boots and bandages on your horse for your warm-up sessions. Just remember to take these restricted items off before you go in to perform your test. Side reins are permitted only when longeing the horse. You can also use a standard longeing whip for this purpose. If you aren't sure about what you can or can't use, find out ahead of time, before it's time to warm up.

The rules also require that the competition number be worn on the bridle whenever the horse is being ridden or exercised. Failure to do so can result in elimination.

When It's Time to Ride Your Test

You and your horse are all warmed up and ready to go. Now what? Check with the ring steward to verify how many other riders are still ahead of you. Things sometimes fall behind schedule at a show, or riders may scratch, so you need to stay informed and flexible.

If things are running on time, watch the clock and arrive at the in-gate a little ahead of your scheduled test time. Wait for the other competitor to finish and exit the arena (see the figure on the next page). If you have someone with you, ask that person to assist with any last-minute grooming touch-ups. For example, while you are mounted, have your helper wipe the dust off your boots with a rag so they will be shiny and clean when you enter the competition arena.

Once the other competitor exits, the ring steward will tell you when it's okay to go in. This short one- or two-minute period between tests, before the judge rings the bell for the next one, gives you an opportunity to ride around the outside of the competition perimeter and get your bearings.

Keep your horse moving well forward, but allow him to have a good look at the judge's box, flower arrangements, spectator stands, vehicles, and anything else that might give him cause to spook. Ride past the judge's box so that the occupants can see your competitor number. Both the judge and the scribe check the numbers against their paperwork to verify that they will be scoring the correct competitor.

Enter at A

When the judge sounds the whistle or bell, you have forty-five seconds to enter the actual competition area and begin your test. (Before 2003, competitors were allowed one minute to enter.) Remember, entering too late is cause for elimination.

A dressage test begins when you enter at A and ends when you give your final salute. All of your practice at home should pay off here as you turn down the center line, without undershooting or overshooting it (common mistakes) and proceed straight toward C, halting squarely at X to give your first salute. When the judge acknowledges, move forward energetically.

A horse that is moving forward well and energetically should feel like he's just on the verge of breaking into the next faster gait.

A well-turned out team await their turn to enter the arena.

For example, a horse at the walk should not amble or shuffle along, but should feel like he's right on the edge of a trot. Of course, he's never supposed to offer the trot until the rider asks for it, but ideally the energy for it should be there for you to tap instantly, with the lightest of aids.

Remember, you cannot cluck to your horse or use your voice at all during a test. You must signal him silently with your other aids. Don't be afraid to use the whip tactfully if he is sucking back or being inattentive to your aids. You cannot speak to your reader, if you're using one, or to anyone on the sidelines. The possibility of not being able to hear your reader is one more good reason to commit your test to memory.

Ride Flawless Figures

Nearly all tests have circles in them somewhere. A twenty-meter circle is the full width of the arena and may be executed at either end or in the middle, depending on the test. You kiss the track on either side, but your horse should stay bent on the arc of the circle at all times, not falling in or drifting out. The judge is looking for a circle that is truly round, not oval or lopsided, and that the horse is balanced and on the aids. The judge is also looking for straightness on the circle, which sounds contradictory when circling, but a horse is traveling straight on the arc when his back feet follow the same tracks as his front feet.

As you navigate the long sides and short sides of the arena, use the corners and half-halts as needed to rebalance your horse, but don't ride too deeply into them. By now, you should be able to coordinate your outside aids with your inside aids well enough to keep the horse from drifting through turns.

When crossing a diagonal, think ahead and plan your turn onto the track so that you don't get jammed up into the corner. Paying attention to little details like this when you ride can mean the difference between a so-so test and a really good one.

Stay Calm, Even If Things Go Wrong

Transitions must be smooth and appear effortless, demonstrating the horse's complete obedience to his rider. Think ahead and prepare for each movement. If your horse breaks gait or takes the wrong canter lead, correct him as quickly as possible without making a big deal about it. Mistakes happen, and the best way to handle them is simply to go on with your test. Don't let yourself come unglued for the rest of the test because something didn't go right. Put it behind you and focus on making the next movement as perfect as possible.

Try not to freeze either, if things are not going as well as you'd hoped. Horses can sense when you're timid or nervous, so if you allow these emotions to creep in, it will only make the situation worse. That's why building confidence is such an important part of classical riding. Ride boldly and bravely, and finish the test with as much finesse as you can muster.

There's nothing in the test that you haven't already practiced at least a hundred times at home, so face it with that mind-set. Riding well is part resolve, part practice. Simply make up your mind that you're going to do it, and then do it. Commit yourself to whatever training and preparation it takes to get there. A test is just a measure of your progress, nothing more.

The Final Halt and Salute

A test ends with your final salute to the judge. Make the last halt a good one, not a hurried or sloppy affair. This is your last chance to impress the judge, so ride it well to the end and leave the arena with a smile on your face. Whether you win or not, you've just accomplished something that many people wish they could do. Go home and feel good about that.

As you leave the arena, the ring steward may ask you to stop so she can check your horse's bit and whip. At some point during a recognized show, you may also be asked to submit your horse to a blood or urine screening test for drugs. This will be carried out by a veterinarian. Failure to cooperate is a violation. Unfortunately, these checks are necessary in today's world to make sure competitors comply with the rules.

Unless you will be riding another test very soon, untack your horse, rub him down, and cool him out. Weather permitting, sponge or hose off the sweat and wipe your tack clean. Give your horse lots of praise and a treat for his effort and hard work. After he's cooled down, don't forget to provide him with plenty of water to keep him well hydrated.

Check Your Score

When the class closes and the scores are posted, go see how you did. If you placed in the ribbons, and an awards ceremony will be held, stay dressed and tacked up so you can accept your award, as shown in the figure on the next page. If no awards ceremony is announced, simply pick up your ribbon afterward.

Happily relaxing after a blue ribbon test.

You may not be able to pick up your test sheet until you turn in your competitor number, but when you do, take time to read the judge's comments. Even if you thought your test went pretty well, don't be surprised if you see some variation of the more common comments, as in this short sampling:

"rushed"

"needs more inside leg"

"could be more forward"

"needs more impulsion"

"abrupt turn at E"

"turn too shallow"

"above the bit"

"on the forehand"

"O [circle] too small"

"shorten reins to better facilitate corners"

Don't be insulted by the comments. The judge is supposed to tell you what you did wrong so that you can improve and advance in your training. Also, the judge only marks what she sees during the test, not what she thinks you or the horse are capable of. Take the information given, discuss it with your instructor or trainer, and practice more on it at home.

Keep all your test sheets for future reference, so that you can compare them to later tests and gauge how well you've progressed. You'll also need to keep them for your records if you're pursuing any kind of year-end awards. The important thing about dressage competition is not the score, and not the ribbons, but whether you come away from the experience having learned something that you can apply to your everyday riding and to your overall enjoyment of your horse.

Chapter Ten

Moving Up and Learning More

Moving Up the Levels

How do you know when you're ready to move up a level in dressage competition? Instructors hear this question all the time from their students, and are, of course, the best judge of when you're ready to move on. To assess your own progress, however, read the *Directives* at the front of each dressage test. These are the instructions on the test sheet that tell you what qualities are being sought and evaluated in each test. Do you and your horse fulfill those requirements? If not, then you still need more work in that level.

Training Level

Training Level, for example, is where you establish the working gaits and confirm that the horse is supple and moving freely forward on contact with good rhythm. Many people don't get the freely forward movement required of a working gait. *Working* gait means just that, the horse and rider are working and covering ground, as if going somewhere with a purpose, not just ambling around the arena with no impulsion.

Of all the gaits, the walk is the one that you can improve the least and is rarely shown to its best advantage. This is because riders don't push their horses forward enough and, instead, allow the horse to plod along or drag a bit. But the walk should be big and marching, with equal intervals between each step. The walk should be animated enough so that the horse appears to be just on the verge of breaking into a trot.

However, be careful not to rush the horse around the arena. There can be a fine line between a good working gait and rushing. If you feel your horse rushing, give a little rein and sit more quietly in the saddle. Make sure you aren't digging in with a spur. Your instructor can help you discern whether you're rushing, until you can feel it yourself. With the walk and all other gaits, you have to find the tempo or speed that shows off the horse's gaits to its best advantage, and this varies for each individual horse.

A horse must be schooling at least at First Level to show well at Training Level. However, at some larger recognized shows, you'll often find horses showing at Training Level that are already schooling at home at Third or Fourth Level. These horses are easy to spot because they move in a more collected frame, which indicates that they are more advanced in their training. The frame expected at Training Level is generally more stretched over the horse's top line, because the horse is not yet required to be fully collected at this stage. (See the figure on the next page, right.)

At schooling shows, you are more likely to find horses showing at a certain level that are not yet confirmed at that level. This is because the rider is trying out a test at that level for practice before attempting it at a recognized show.

Transitions are a good gauge of your progress and readiness to move on. For example, do you allow your horse to dump onto his forehand (also shown in the figure on the next page, left) when transitioning downward from canter to trot? If you do, you need more practice. Training Level horses aren't required to be fully collected, but they shouldn't move on the forehand either. To prevent your horse from falling on the forehand during the transition, give a little with your hands, because the horse's neck has to come down a little to make the transition. At the same time, keep your body position upright and slightly back, and use your legs and seat to drive the horse from behind into the bridle. The driving aids keep the horse off the forehand; you cannot hold him off the forehand by pulling back on the reins.

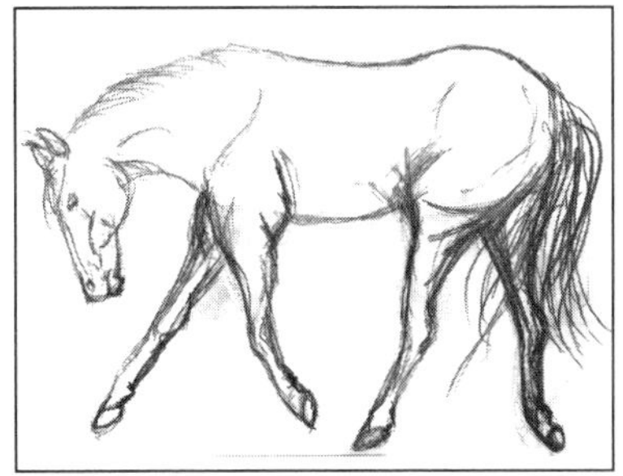

A horse on the forehand (left) and a horse that is moving well in a proper, balanced frame for his level of training (right).

Because transitions are a good indicator of the quality of training, they receive a great deal of emphasis in today's dressage tests. So do not neglect your attention to details in this area, or your scores will suffer.

First Level

Thrust, or pushing power, distinguishes First Level from Training Level. The horse is more collected at this level, but you still show him at the working gaits, in addition to the lengthened and medium gaits. A lengthened trot, for example, is pushed out with more extension in the stride, while the medium trot is a more uphill, more collected, and more together movement than the working gait.

The horse has to show clear transitions from the working gait into the lengthened strides and back down into the working gait again, all while maintaining tempo. He should not merely speed up into the lengthening and then slow down again when returning to a working gait. Dressage is about controlled power, and the quality of these gaits and transitions demonstrates the rider's precision as he pushes the horse out into a lengthened stride and brings him back.

Second Level

In Second Level, the horse demonstrates that he is developing collection by accepting more of his weight on the hindquarters.

The best training for this carriage is the shoulder-in. Second Level also asks for travers (see the figure on this page), renvers, and simple changes of lead.

In the change of canter lead through the walk, the horse transitions to the walk (without falling on the forehand) and takes three to five quiet steps at the walk (no trot steps) before striking off into the other canter lead. The rider should keep the horse straight while at the walk.

Third Level

At Third Level, you've achieved the thrust required in Second Level, and now you're improving collection by getting the horse to lift and push more, and polishing performance with cadence and suspension. Cadence is the accentuation of a gait, while suspension adds more brilliance to the gait. Third Level also introduces the extended paces, half-pass, and single flying changes. The extended gaits are not intended to just let the horse "go like hell," but are designed to allow him to stretch more over his top line, while demonstrating his controlled power.

Travers, or haunches-in, is the opposite of shoulder-in.

At Third Level, you can also use a full bridle. A full bridle has two bits, a curb and snaffle. The curb bit works on the horse's tongue, and the snaffle works on the bars of the horse's mouth. A full bridle allows the rider to use more tact and less force than with just the single snaffle bit. The hands can have a quieter connection. The connection on both sets of reins should be equal, and the rider shouldn't feel one bit in the horse's mouth more than the other, for most situations. Used correctly, both a full bridle and spurs, which are an artificial extension of the leg aids, enable the rider to whisper his aids, instead of shouting.

Fourth Level

Fourth Level demonstrates a high degree of all the qualities achieved in the previous levels—rhythm, suppleness, contact, impulsion, straightness, and collection. These qualities must be well honed before attempting more difficult maneuvers, such as the pirouettes and tempi changes introduced at this level. Movements are energetic and transitions are smooth and precise. Like well-acquainted dance partners, horse and rider move together as one, in beautiful harmony.

Riding to Music

Perhaps the most beautiful, artistic expression of the harmony between horse and rider is the musical freestyle (called *kur* in German), always a spectator favorite at shows. Even people who don't know anything about the dressage movements can appreciate this lovely equine ballet set to music.

Musical freestyle, which is an excellent way to enhance your enjoyment of the dressage experience, gives you an opportunity to design your own test and be creative and original within the context of classical riding. Freestyle tests can be performed at any level. You may choose your own music and choreograph and incorporate all the movements required at the level at which you will perform the freestyle. You cannot perform any movements above your chosen level.

Costumed musical freestyle is fun for exhibitors and popular with spectators. Here, Marie Klimchuk portrays Zorro on Braveheart.

The rider selects music that complements the rhythm and tempo of his horse's gaits. Generally, when combining several pieces of music, the rider tries to create a coherent theme. Classical music, of course, is a favorite background for showing off the classical riding movements; however, riders have used jazz, swing, ragtime, rock 'n' roll, Latin compositions, and other genres for their themes.

Most freestyles are performed under the same traditional dress codes as regular dressage tests. However, some shows arrange specially designated costume freestyle classes, in which the horse and rider dress up to match their musical theme. These are especially popular with spectators and serve to generate greater interest in dressage. See the figure on this page.

All the movements in a freestyle test must still be technically accurate, just as in a regular dressage test, but you are not required to execute them in the same place or in the same sequence as the regular test. You can use the entire arena and be creative with where and when you execute figures, patterns, and movements. This is your opportunity to apply some artistic expression to the sport, show off what your horse does best, and minimize his weaker points.

The Quadrille

Something else to try your hand at after you gain a little riding experience is a quadrille. Popular among youth riders, but suitable for any age group, a *quadrille* is a team of four riders who execute dressage movements together as a cohesive unit. With a history rooted in the cavalry, many public quadrille exhibitions still emphasize military themes. Among the most famous quadrille teams are the Royal Canadian Mounted Police and the white Lipizzan stallions of the Spanish Riding School in Vienna, Austria.

Whether performing in competition or exhibitions, in traditional dress or in costume, participation in a quadrille is more than just fun. It offers the camaraderie of other like-minded riders and an excellent opportunity for improving your riding skills. Teams can compete with standardized tests and freestyles, with compulsory movements required in each of five levels. Spectators often find the complex drill precision of a quadrille team more

The Pas de Deux

Similar to the quadrille, the pas de deux is an artistic program for two riders to present their horses to best advantage in a musical freestyle context. The two riders enter the ring as a pair, execute any combination of figures, patterns, and transitions related to their chosen level, and then exit the arena together. There are no compulsory movements that the duo must include in their program, and they cannot perform movements that are higher than the level at which they are entered. Like the quadrille, the pas de deux is an enriching and educational experience in precision teamwork and concentration.

awe inspiring than a solo musical freestyle, so they are a good way to attract interest in the sport.

The Learner-Judge Program

Have you ever wondered why judges consistently score some horse-and-rider teams higher than others? If you're going to compete in dressage, it helps to understand what the judge is looking for. Better yet, you need to learn to think like a judge.

The U.S. Dressage Federation (USDF) "L" Education Program for Judge Training is the first step toward becoming a licensed judge. The L stands for *Learning*, as in *learner-judge*. Even if you have no real aspirations to become a full-fledged horse show judge, you can audit this program and learn what judges know. It is an excellent educational opportunity for all serious adult dressage riders to consider, should a program be offered near your vicinity. Take advantage of it, if a program is offered near your area, because the knowledge you'll gain will be an asset throughout your dressage career.

Designed to teach participants to evaluate dressage performance from Training through Second Levels, the "L" program can help you become a more savvy rider and competitor. You'll study all the dressage basics: gaits, movements, figures, patterns, terminology, plus musical freestyle, equine biomechanics, competition rules, scoring methodology, and much more.

The program is divided into five sessions, A, B, C, and D, plus a final exam, spaced a month or so apart. Each session usually takes place over a weekend, and is set up in lecture format, with demonstrations often included. The program concludes with a final exam, which auditors do not take. Auditors also do not attend the D session.

As an auditor, you aren't required to meet the prerequisites that participants aiming to become judges must fulfill. Also, the cost varies for participants and auditors, depending on the location and the host organization.

The L program can significantly increase your dressage knowledge and help you develop a discerning eye for good riding and training. Plus, you'll meet judges and other committed dressage enthusiasts with whom you can network and share experiences. Your time invested in the program is guaranteed to be well worth the effort. To find out if there's an "L" program offered near you, visit the USDF Web site at www.usdf.org and look under "Education."

When Sport Becomes Art

The purest traditions of classical riding are preserved and performed by the famous Lipizzaners of the Spanish Riding School. These magnificent stallions and their riders truly elevate dressage to its highest art, called *haute ecole*. The spectacular leaps, called airs above the ground, for which the stallions are so famous are not part of today's competition dressage tests, but they are part of the rich history and tradition of classical training. Said to have originated from evasive maneuvers executed by war horses and their riders, when combat was once waged on horseback, the airs were often exhibited with great pageantry for European royalty and the upper classes in centuries past.

The airs above the ground include the levade, the courbette, the capriole, and the croupade. At the Spanish Riding School in Vienna, Austria, only stallions are trained to perform these difficult and demanding maneuvers, which may be performed under saddle or on the long lines without a rider.

- **Levade:** The airs stem from this maneuver, which is basically a balanced, controlled rear. The horse raises up on its haunches and holds his position at a 45-degree angle to the ground. Normally, when a horse rears straight up, he is in grave danger of falling over backward with his rider, because his stance on two hind legs is precarious and unbalanced. That's what makes the levade, which requires great balance, strength, and conditioning to execute with perfect control, so difficult and astonishing.
- **Courbette:** From a balanced levade, the horse executes a series of jumps on his hind legs.

- **Capriole:** In this maneuver, the horse leaps into the air, with forelegs tucked to his chest, and kicks out behind with his hind legs.
- **Croupade:** Similar to the capriole, except when the horse leaps into the air, he keeps both the front legs and the hind legs tucked under his body.

Today, every horseman who studies classical riding is helping to preserve an ancient art and tradition. We owe our horses the best and fairest treatment and training we can provide, for horses have carried humans far in our history, conquering lands and settling nations. They've also suffered greatly at our hands for their role in building civilization.

Fortunately, horses today are more widely regarded as companion animals, rather than mere beasts of burden. But the bond we establish with them differs markedly from the bond we might build with a cat or dog. This is because horses are bigger and stronger than we are. We know they can hurt us, and they know it, too. Thus, the bond we seek to establish through classical training is a partnership based on mutual respect, not fear. We seek to understand the horse, while respecting his superior size and strength. When treated fairly and rewarded for his efforts, the horse comes to respect us and trust our leadership authority. The act of classical riding becomes a joyful and pleasurable experience shared by both partners, who relish the opportunity to stretch and flex and enjoy the pure physicality of being alive in the moment. This sharing, a sort of harmony of hearts held by two different species, is a thing of beauty that defies description and is an art unto itself. Call it *art*, or, if you will, call it *love*, for whatever it is, it involves the miracle of joining two bodies, two hearts, and two minds into a dance of mutual trust and respect, ultimately bringing out the best in both participants.

Glossary of Common Horse Terms

above the bit A movement by a horse to evade contact with the bit by raising his head and sticking his muzzle forward, so that his mouth and the bit are above a rider's hands.

action The way a horse moves at the various gaits; a horse's way of going.

aids The signals used by a rider to communicate with a horse and tell him what to do.

airs above the ground Advanced *haute ecole* (high school) movements and controlled leaps off the ground preserved and performed for exhibition, primarily by the Lipizzaners of Spanish Riding School fame.

barn sour Used to describe an undesirable, acquired trait of a horse who refuses to leave the vicinity of his stable and herd companions without becoming difficult to handle or trying to turn and flee back to the barn while being ridden away.

bend The arc from head to tail on a horse's body as it curves around a rider's inside leg; bending of the neck only is incorrect. (Note: The rider's *inside leg* is always relative to the bend of the horse, regardless of what side the rail is on.)

bolting A horse's attempt to run away from his rider, whether from genuine fright or deliberate misbehavior.

bolting feed An undesirable habit of horses to eat too quickly without thoroughly chewing food; can lead to choke and digestive problems.

bot fly A parasitic insect that lays tiny, yellow eggs on a horse's hair, usually on the legs, gets ingested, and continues its life cycle inside the horse.

broodmare A female horse used for breeding purposes.

buck To put the head down low, arch the back, and leap into the air off all four legs or lift only the hind end off the ground.

bute The nickname for phenylbutazone, a common anti-inflammatory drug used to control pain and inflammation in horses.

caller, reader A person who reads a dressage test aloud for the rider; certain events do not permit callers.

cadence The accentuation of a gait relating to the tempo and the springiness of a horse's steps.

capriole One of the more spectacular airs above the ground in which a horse leaps off the ground and, with the body mostly horizontal to the ground, kicks out with the hind legs.

cavalletti Poles laid on the ground and evenly spaced at a precise distance used for schooling and correcting certain problems.

Concours Dresseur International (CDI) An international dressage competition; CDI-W indicates that the event is a World Cup qualifier.

choke A condition in which partially chewed food lodges in a horse's esophagus, making it impossible for him to swallow.

closing date The last date that a horse show entry form can be postmarked for acceptance; after this date, entries are called post entries and may or may not be accepted.

collective marks Scores at the bottom of a dressage test sheet that cover a horse's gaits, impulsion, and submission and a rider's seat, position, and effectiveness of the aids.

Coggins test A test used to rule out equine infectious anemia, a highly contagious equine disease; a negative test result is required with horse show entries and interstate transportation of horses.

coldblooded horse A heavy draft horse bred for working.

collection The gathering together of a horse with his hind legs under his body to provide maximum impulsion; causes his outline to appear shorter overall and higher in front and his strides to be shorter and higher.

colic A stomach ache or digestive upset in a horse; gastrointestinal disturbances or blockages that can range from mild to severe and life threatening.

colt A young male horse under 4 years of age.

cooling out The time spent after a workout walking a horse and allowing him time to relax and cool off gradually.

contact The elastic connection through the reins from a rider's hands to a horse's mouth.

counter-canter A canter in which a horse leads with the outside foreleg; perhaps more plainly explained as deliberately cantering on the wrong lead relative to a horse's direction.

counter-change of hand A zigzag half-pass in which a horse moves from the center line toward the rail and back toward the center line, or vice versa.

dam A horse's mother.

directives Instructions on the dressage test sheet that describe the purpose of the test and the qualities of movement and training being tested.

easy keeper A horse that easily keeps weight on without having to eat extra feed; in contrast, a hard keeper requires more feed to keep weight on.

engagement An ingredient of collection and impulsion that refers more to the weight-carrying capacity of the hind legs, their increased flexion, and their ability to step well under a horse and support his weight, rather than their pushing power.

Federation Equestre Internationale (FEI) The international governing body of equestrian competition that is responsible for writing and regulating the international level dressage tests.

filly A young female horse less than 4 years old.

flake The common measurement for a section of hay pulled off the bale; a single bale of hay divides into about ten flakes.

flexion The bending of a horse's head at the poll (highest point of the head) without showing tension in the neck or jaws; a horse may also be flexed toward his direction of travel or against his direction (counter-flexion).

flexion test A test a veterinarian uses to check for soundness in a horse. The vet flexes and holds the horse's leg for a minute, then has someone lead off the horse at a trot to check for lameness.

flying change At the canter, a horse jumps from one leading leg to the other, switching leads in midair.

foal A baby horse.

frame The outline of a horse relative to the degree of extension or collection.

free walk A pace that allows a horse to relax, lower his head, and stretch out his neck. A rider feeds out the reins as the horse stretches down but maintains contact.

gallop A horse's fastest gait, similar to the canter but at greater speed and covering more ground. There are usually four beats to the gallop whereas a correct canter has three beats.

gatekeeper A person, usually a volunteer, assigned to open and close the dressage arena gate for each competitor at a horse show.

gelding A male horse that has been castrated.

green horse A horse that has had little or no training or experience at being ridden.

half-halt A slight checking or collection of the movement used in any pace, often to rebalance a horse, get his attention, or prepare him for any change or new command.

half-pass A forward and sideways movement in which a horse is bent toward his direction of travel.

impulsion The freely forward moving energy that comes from a horse pushing or driving himself from the hindquarters, instead of dragging himself from the forehand.

lateral work Refers to the forward and sideways dressage movements in which a horse's feet step along two or more tracks.

leg-yield A sideways movement in which a horse moves off the rider's leg and is flexed away from his direction of travel.

mare An adult female horse over 4 years old.

on the aids A commonly used phrase indicating that a horse is well connected, on the bit, and responding appropriately to a rider's commands.

on the forehand, heavy on the forehand A horse carries most of his weight on the front legs and front half of his body, giving a downhill appearance to his movements.

passage A slow, cadenced trot having a moment of suspension between steps.

piaffe A highly collected cadenced trot on the spot; trot in place.

pirouette A turn in which a horse's forehand makes a half (half-pirouette) or full circle around his hind legs, usually performed at walk or canter.

port A bend or curve in the center of a curb bit that allows room for a horse's tongue.

rein-back The term for backing up straight, stepping with diagonal pairs of legs.

ring steward A person, often a volunteer, assigned to keep entries moving on schedule and let dressage competitors know how many rides are still ahead of their test time; this person may also check equipment.

runner A person, usually a volunteer, assigned at a horse show to retrieve test sheets from the judge and carry them back to the show office for processing.

scribe A person, usually a volunteer, who sits beside the judge at a dressage show and records her marks and comments on each competitor's test sheet.

scorer A person, usually a volunteer, who calculates the dressage competitors' test scores.

soundness Being of good health, good condition, and free of any lameness. A horse is said to be sound when in this condition.

stallion An intact adult male horse over 4 years of age, capable of breeding.

straightness The horse's forehand moves square in front of the hindquarters; even on a curved line the horse is bent in the turn but is said to be straight when the hind feet tread into the hoofprints of the forefeet, and not falling out to either side of the forehand.

technical delegate (TD) A horse show official who represents the governing body, acts as an advisor, and makes sure that the rules are followed.

throughness Describes a state of supple connectedness in which a circuit of energy flows freely from a horse's hindquarters through his top line to the bit, then back through the reins to a rider, whose aids influence the hindquarters and keep the energy going.

tracking up A desirable quality of stride in which a horse's hind feet step into the tracks of his forefeet; in overtracking, the hind feet step in front of the prints left by the forefeet, which is desirable in extended paces.

turn on the forehand A horse moves his hind legs in a half or full circle, pivoting around a foreleg.

turn on the haunches Starting from a halt and being ridden at the walk, a horse moves his forehand around the hind legs; when performed correctly, the front legs cross over each other and the hind legs step with the turn but remain at the pivotal spot.

uberstreichen A German dressage term describing the momentary release of the reins, during which the rider reaches forward over a horse's neck and rides for several strides on a slack rein to determine if she is correctly carrying herself and on the aids.

U.S. Equestrian Team (USET) An organization that selects American riders to compete internationally for world championships and Olympic teams.

weanling A young horse of either sex, less than 1 year old, that has been weaned.

yearling A young horse of either sex that is 1 year old.

References

Books

Belasik, Paul. *Dressage for the 21st-Century.* North Pomfret, Vt.: Trafalgar Square Publishing, 2001.

Budiansky, Stephen. *The Nature of Horses: Exploring Equine Evolution, Intelligence, and Behavior.* New York: Free Press, 1997.

Burkhardt, Barbara. *Dressage from A to X: The Definitive Guide to Riding and Competing.* North Pomfret, Vt.: Trafalgar Square Publishing, 2004.

Crossley, Anthony. *Advanced Dressage: A Companion to Training the Young Horse: The First Two Years.* London: Stanley Paul, 1982.

———. *Training the Young Horse: The First Two Years.* London: Stanley Paul, 1987.

de Kunffy, Charles. *The Athletic Development of the Dressage Horse. Manege Patterns.* New York: Howell Book House, 1992.

———. *Dressage Principles Illuminated.* North Pomfret, Vt.: Trafalgar Square Publishing, 2002.

de la Gueriniere, Francois Robichon. *Ecole de Cavalerie.* Cleveland Heights, Ohio: Xenophon Press, 1992.

de Ruffieu, Francois Lemaire. *The Handbook of Riding Essentials.* New York: Harper & Row, 1986.

Evans, J. Warren, Anthony Borton, Harold Hintz, and L. Dale Van Vleck. *The Horse.* New York: W. H. Freeman, 1999.

Fraser, Suzanne K. B. *The Dressage Competitors' Handbook.* Meriden, N.H.: Equissentials Press, 1999.

Gahwyler, Max. *The Competitive Edge: Improving Your Scores in the Lower Levels.* Boonsboro, Md.: Half Halt Press, 1995.

———. *The Competitive Edge II: Moving up the Levels.* Boonsboro, Md.: Half Halt Press, 1992.

———. *The Competitive Edge III: Gravity, Balance, and Kinetics of the Horse and Rider.* Boonsboro, Md.: Half Halt Press, 2000.

German National Equestrian Federation. *Advanced Techniques of Dressage.* Translated by Christina Belton. Addington, UK: Kenilworth Press, 2003.

———. *The Principles of Riding.* Translated by Christina Belton. Addington, UK: Kenilworth Press, 2003.

Guay, Mary, and Donna Schlinkert. *Buying Your First Horse: A Comprehensive Guide to Preparing for, Finding, and Purchasing a Great Horse.* Marietta, Ga.: White Papers Press, 1997.

Haas, Jessie. *Safe Horse, Safe Rider: A Young Rider's Guide to Responsible Horsekeeping.* Pownal, Vt.: Storey Books, 1994.

Hamilton, Kate. *Dressage: An Approach to Competition.* New York: Howell Book House, 1988.

Harris, Moira C. *Dressage by the Letter: A Guide for the Novice.* New York: Howell Book House, 1997.

Harris, Susan E. *The United States Pony Club Manual of Horsemanship* (editions for Basic, Intermediate, and Advanced Horsemanship). New York: Howell Book House, 1996.

Henriquet, Michel, and Catherine Durand. *Henriquet on Dressage.* North Pomfret, Vt.: Trafalgar Square Publishing, 2004.

Herbermann, Erik. *Dressage Formula.* London: J. A. Allen, 1980.

Hillsdon, Penny. Pathfinder Dressage: *The Philosophy and Training Techniques of the World's Top Trainers.* London: J. A. Allen, 2000.

Kidd, Jane. *Dressage Essentials: Takes the Mystery out of the Fastest Growing Equestrian Discipline.* New York: Howell Book House, 1999.

Kyrkland, Kyra, and Jytte Lemkow. *Dressage with Kyra: The Kyra Kyrklund Training Method.* North Pomfret, Vt.: Trafalgar Square Publishing, 1998.

Lang, Amanda. *Rider's Handbook.* New York: Sterling Publishing, 2002.

Ljungquist, Bengt. *Practical Dressage Manual.* Boonsboro, Md.: Half Halt Press, 1976.

Loch, Sylvia. *The Classical Rider: Being at One with Your Horse.* North Pomfret, Vt.: Trafalgar Square Publishing, 2000.

———. *The Classical Seat: A Guide for the Everyday Rid*er. *Horse & Rider*. London: D. J. Murphy, 2002.

———. *Dressage and the Art of Classical Riding.* North Pomfret, Vt.: Trafalgar Square Publishing, 2001.

———. *Dressage in Lightness: Speaking the Horse's Language.* North Pomfret, Vt.: Trafalgar Square Publishing, 2000.

———. Invisible Riding. *The Secret of Balance for You and Your Horse.* London: Horse's Mouth, 2003.

Loriston-Clarke, Jennie. *The Complete Guide to Dressage: How to Achieve Perfect Harmony between You and Your Horse.* Philadelphia: Running Press, 1987.

Mills, Daniel, and Kathryn Nankervis. *Equine Behaviour: Principles and Practice.* London: Blackwell Science, 1999.

Museler, Wilhelm. *Riding Logic.* New York: Arco Publishing, 1984.

Nelson, Hilda, and Francois Baucher. *The Man and His Method.* London: J. A. Allen, 1992.

O'Connor, Sally. *Common Sense Dressage: An Illustrated Guide.* Middletown, Md.: Half Halt Press, 1990.

Oliveira, Nuno. *Reflections on Equestrian Art.* London: J. A. Allen, 2001.

Podhajsky, Alois. *The Complete Training of Horse and Rider in the Principles of Classical Horsemanship.* Garden City, N.Y.: Doubleday, 1967.

———. *My Horses, My Teachers.* North Pomfret, Vt.: Trafalgar Square Publishing, 1997.

———. *The Riding Teacher.* North Pomfret, Vt.: Trafalgar Square Publishing, 2004.

Savoie, Jane. *It's Not Just about the Ribbons.* North Pomfret, Vt.: Trafalgar Square Publishing, 2003.

Siegal, Mordecai, editor. *UC Davis School of Veterinary Medicine Book of Horses: A Complete Medical Reference Guide for Horses and Foals.* New York: HarperCollins Publishers, 1996.

Sivewright, Molly. *Thinking Riding: Training Student Instructors.* London: J. A. Allen, 1979.

———. *Thinking Riding Book 2: In Good Form.* London: J. A. Allen, 1984.

Swift, Sally. *Centered Riding.* North Pomfret, Vt.: Trafalgar Square Publishing, 1985.

U.S. Dressage Federation. *Classical Training of the Horse.* Lincoln, Neb.: U.S. Dressage Federation, 1998.

Von Ziegner, Kurd Albrecht. *The Elements of Dressage: A Guide for Training the Young Horse.* Guilford, Conn.: Lyons Press, 2002.

Winnett, John. *Dressage as Art in Competition: Blending Classical and Competitive Riding.* Guilford, Conn.: Lyons Press, 1993.

Worth, Melyni. *Storey's Guide to Feeding Horses.* North Adams, Mass.: Storey Publishing, 2003.

Horse Magazines

Dressage Today
PRIMEDIA Enthusiast Publications, Inc.
P.O. Box 420235
Palm Coast, FL 32142-0235
(800) 877-5396
E-mail: dressage@palmcoastd.com
Web site: dressagetoday.com

Equus
PRIMEDIA Enthusiast Publications, Inc.
(800) 829-5910 or (386) 447-6332
E-mail: Equus@Palmcoastd.com
Web site: Equusmagazine.com

The Horse
Blood-Horse Publications
(800) 582-5604
E-mail: Subscribe@TheHorse.com

Horse Illustrated
Fancy Publications
P.O. Box 57549
Boulder, CO 80322
(800) 365-4421
E-mail: fancy@neodata.com and enter "Horse Illustrated" in subject field

Horse of Kings Magazine
HOK
P.O. Box 110545
Palm Bay, FL 32911-0545
(321) 288-0235

USDF Connection
Official publication of the U.S. Dressage Federation
220 Lexington Green Circle, Suite 510
Lexington, KY 40503
(859) 971-2277
Web site: www.usdf.org

National Dressage Organizations

Dressage at Devon
Highest rated international dressage competition outside of Europe, held annually in Devon, PA, organized and presented by the Delaware Valley Combined Training Association.
Web site: www.dressageatdevon.org

Federation Equestre Internationale (FEI), the International Federation of Equestrian Sport
Avenue Mon-Repos 24, CH-1000
Lausanne 5, Switzerland
Web site: www.horsesport.org

U.S. Dressage Federation, Inc. (USDF)
220 Lexington Green Circle, Suite 510
Lexington, KY 40503
(859) 971-2277
Web site: www.usdf.org

U.S. Equestrian Federation (USEF)
4047 Iron Works Parkway
Lexington, KY 40511-8483
(859) 258-2472
Web site: www.usef.org

Local Dressage Organizations

Whether you live in Canada, Hawaii, or Alaska, there's probably a dressage association near you. If you don't know how to locate one, the U.S. Dressage Federation maintains a list of dressage clubs and chapters on its Web site at www.usdf.org under GMOs, for group-member organizations. The following is a partial listing to help you find a dressage organization in your area:

Alamo Dressage Association
www.alamodressage.org

Alaska Dressage Association
www.alaskadressage.org

Aloha State Dressage Society
www.alohastatedressage.com

Arizona Dressage Association
www.azdressage.org

Arkansas Dressage Society
www.arkansasdressage.org

Big Sky Equestrian Association
www.bigskyequestrian.org

Birmingham Dressage and Combined Training Association
www.bdcta.org

California Dressage Society
www.california-dressage.org

Central Florida Dressage
www.centralfloridadressage.com

Central New York Dressage and Combined Training Association
www.cnydcta.org

Central States Dressage and Eventing Association
www.csdea.org

Central Texas Society
www.CenTexDressage.org

Central Vermont Dressage Association
www.cvda.org

Central Washington Dressage Society
www.centralwashingtondressage.org

Chattanooga Dressage and Combined Training Association
www.chattdcta.freeservers.com

Commonwealth Dressage and Combined Training Association
www.cdcta.com

Connecticut Dressage Association
www.ctdressageassoc.org

Dakota Dressage and Eventing
www.yahoogroups.com/group/dakdressage

Dallas Dressage Club
www.dallasdressage.org

Deep South Dressage and Combined Training Association
www.dsdcta.org

Delaware Valley Combined Training Association
www.dvcta.org

Delta Dressage Association
www.deltadressage.com

Dressage Association of Southern California
www.dressageassn.com

East Coast Regional Dressage Association
www.ecrda.com

East Tennessee Combined Training and Dressage Association
www.etctda.org

Eastern Iowa Dressage and Eventing Association
www.mwnet.com/eidea

Eastern New York Dressage and Combined Training
www.enydcta.org

Eastern States Dressage and Combined Training Association
www.esdcta.org

Edmonton Area Alberta Dressage
www.albertadressage.com/eaada/eaindex.htm

Fort Worth Dressage Club
www.fortworthdressage.com

Georgia Dressage and Combined Training Association
www.gdcta.org

Gold Coast Dressage Association
www.gcdafl.org

Houston Dressage Society
www.houstondressagesociety.org

Illinois Dressage and Combined Training Association
www.idcta.org

Indiana Dressage Association
www.midwestdressage.org

Iowa Dressage and Combined Training Association
www.iadcta.tripod.com

Kentucky Dressage Association
www.kentuckydressageassociation.org

Lehigh Valley Dressage Association
www.lvda.org

Maine Dressage Society
www.mainedressagesociety.org

Maryland Dressage Association
www.marylandressage.org

Middle Georgia Sport Horse Association
www.mgsha.org

Mid-Ohio Dressage Association
www.midohiodressage.org

Mississippi Eventing and Dressage Association
www.cedarwindfarm.com/MsEDA

Montana Dressage Society
www.montanadressage.org

Nebraska Dressage Association
www.nebraskadressage.org

New England Dressage Association
www.neda.org/~neda

New Mexico Dressage Association
www.members.aol.com/NMDressage

North Carolina Dressage and Combined Training Association
www.ncdcta.com

Northeast Florida Dressage Association
www.nfladressage.org

Northern Ohio Dressage Association
www.nodarider.org

Ohio Dressage Society
www.ohiodressagesociety.com

Oklahoma Dressage Society
www.oklahomadressage.org

Oley Valley Combined Training Association
www.ovcta.org

Orange County Dressage Association
www.dressageunltd.com/ocda

Ozark Dressage Society
www.ozarkdressage.org

Potomac Valley Dressage Association
www.pvda.org

Rocky Mountain Dressage Society
www.rmds.org

St. Louis Area Dressage Society
www.slads.org

South Carolina Dressage and Combined Training Association
www.scdcta.com

Southern Arizona Dressage Association
www.sazda.org

Southern New Hampshire Dressage and Combined Training Association
www.snhdcta.org

Southwest Florida Dressage Association
www.geocities.com/swfda

Southwest Virginia Dressage Association
www.swvada.com

Tennessee Valley Dressage and Combined Training Association
www.tvda.org

Tri-State Dressage Association
www.tri-statedressage.org

Tucson Dressage Club
www.tucsondressageclub.org

Utah Dressage Society
www.utahdressagesociety.org

Virginia Dressage Association
www.vadressage.org

Western New York Dressage Association
www.wnyda.org

Western Pennsylvania Dressage Association
www.wpdadressage.org

Wisconsin Dressage and Combined Training Association
www.wdcta.org

Other Equine Organizations

American Association of Equine Practitioners
4075 Iron Works Pike
Lexington, KY 40511
(859) 233-0147
Web site: www.aaep.org

American Farriers Association
4059 Iron Works Pike
Lexington, KY 40511
(859) 233-7411
Web site: www.americanfarriers.org

American Horse Council
1616 H Street NW, 7th Floor
Washington, DC 20006
(202) 296-4031
E-mail: ahc@horsecouncil.org
Web site: www.horsecouncil.org

American Riding Instructors Association (ARIA)
28801 Trenton Court
Bonita Springs, FL 34124-3337
(239) 948-3232
Web site: www.riding-instructor.com

U.S. Equestrian Team (USET)
P.O. Box 355
Gladstone, NJ 07934
(908) 234-1251
Web site: www.uset.com

U.S. Pony Clubs, Inc.
4041 Iron Works Pike
Lexington, KY 40511
(859) 254-7669
Web site: www.ponyclub.org

World Wide Warmbloods
Web site: wwwarmbloods.com/index.html

Breed Associations and Registries

American Hanoverian Society
4067 Iron Works Parkway
Lexington, KY 40511
(859) 255-4141
Web site: www.hanoverian.org

American Holsteiner Horse Association
222 East Main Street, Suite 1
Georgetown, KY 40324-1712
(502) 863-4239
E-mail: ahhambr@bellsouth.net
Web site: www.holsteiner.com

American Quarter Horse Association
P.O. Box 200
Amarillo, TX 79168
Web site: www.aqha.com

American Trakehner Association
1514 West Church Street
Newark, OH 43055
(740) 344-1111
E-mail: atahorses@alltel.net
Web site: www.americantrakehner.com

The Jockey Club (Thoroughbred registry)
821 Corporate Drive
Lexington, KY 40503-2794
(859) 224-2700
Web site: www.jockeyclub.com

Horse Equipment Catalogs

Back in the Saddle
570 Turner Drive, Suite D
Durango, CO 81303
(800) 865-2478
Web site: www.backinthesaddle.com

Dressage Extensions
27501 Cumberland Road
Tehachapi, CA 93561
(800) 541-3708
Web site: www.dressageextensions.com

SmartPak Equine
40 Grissom Road, #500
Plymouth, MA 02360
(800) 461-8898
Web site: www.SmartPakEquine.com

Stateline Tack, Inc.
1989 Transit Way
P.O. Box 910
Brockport, NY 14420-0910
(800) 228-9208
Web site: www.statelinetack.com

About the Author

Karen Leigh Davis has written numerous books and articles about cats and other companion animals. Her lifelong passion, however, is horses. Davis is a longtime student of dressage. *Deciphering Dressage* is her first attempt at combining four special loves into one project: the love of writing, the love of dressage, the love of horses, and the love of horses in art. Davis drew most of the illustrations for this book.

As a little girl, Davis was enthralled with Marguerite Henry's book *White Stallion of Lipizza,* the story of the Lipizzan stallions of Spanish Riding School fame, which was beautifully illustrated by Wesley Dennis. Davis was inspired by both the story and the art, and it was where she first discovered dressage, although she didn't take up classical riding until adulthood.

Davis feels that taking up dressage as an adult uniquely qualifies her to write about the topic for newcomers to the sport, whether they've ridden in other disciplines or whether they're new to horses altogether. For years, Davis took lessons in other riding disciplines before finding a dressage instructor, and then she found that learning dressage was like having to learn to ride all over again. But the effort was well worth every saddle-sore moment, because Davis enjoys her horses and riding now more than ever before. She hopes this book will help others who are interested in pursuing dressage avoid some of the pitfalls and setbacks that she encountered along the way.

A native of Roanoke, Virginia, Davis owns a Holsteiner schoolmaster and a Hanoverian filly. She has served on the board of the Southwest Virginia Dressage Association.

Index

Index

Index

Index

Index

Index